CONTENTS

Ships in Focus Publications

Correspondence and editorial:
Roy Fenton
18 Durrington Avenue
London SW20 8NT
020 8879 3527
rfenton@rfenton.demon.co.uk

Orders and photographic:
John & Marion Clarkson
18 Franklands, Longton
Preston PR4 5PD
01772 612855
Orders: 0845 0760078
shipsinfocus@btinternet.com

SHIPS IN FOCUS RECORD
ISBN 1 901703 81 9

SUBSCRIPTION RATES FOR RECORD

Readers can start their subscription with any issue, and are welcome to backdate it to receive previous issues.

	3 issues	4 issues
UK	£24	£31
Europe (airmail)	£26	£34
Rest of the world (surface mail)	£26	£34
Rest of the world (airmail)	£31	£41

SHIPS IN FOCUS

Novembe

When we began 'Record' ten years ago, we made a decision which we are now about to reverse. At the time we felt it was inappropriate for us as publishers to review books, and hoped that we could leave this to others. Well, to be frank, we are disappointed by the standard of book reviewing in the popular journals. Too often the reviews are based entirely on the publisher's blurb (we know: we often recognize the blurb we've supplied when reading reviews of our books), and are usually too brief to examine whether the book really makes an original contribution and meets acceptable standards of research, writing and reproduction. From this issue we are going to devote space to reviewing books that we feel our readers would like to be told about or, equally, warned off. Setting aside our original reservations, we are convinced we *can* be objective about the work of other publishers. Indeed, more positively, we think our experience in publishing helps us to recognise books which could have been done better, and are inadequately researched, shoddily edited, poorly compiled, or badly printed. We aim to be critical yet constructive, in the hope of spreading the message about what we believe makes a book good.

We cannot review everything, and will restrict ourselves to a few books in each issue whose subject will, we feel, appeal to 'Record' readers. And we will try to resist the temptation to choose only stinkers. There is a risk we might upset people, but any author or publisher must realize that placing a book in front of the public - just like transmitting a TV programme or putting on a play - renders them open to praise, indifference or disdain, depending on how well they have picked their subject, explored it and performed their job of writer or illustrator. To any author or publisher who feels aggrieved we would point out that this journal does have a correspondence column.

The reviews in this issue are all by one of the editors, but this will not necessarily continue, as we intend to ask others to do reviews, and welcome any sent in, unprompted, by readers.

The feature on Bookers by Andrew Bell in 'Record' 35 has been very well received, readers appreciating the background which Andrew filled in so well. There have been a number of relevant letters, several asking for a fleet list of Booker's smaller vessels working in Guiana, and a major contribution to this list. More work is needed before this is ready for publication, and it will appear, along with other comments on Bookers, in a forthcoming issue.

Due to lack of space, and a desire to keep contributors happy, part two of 'Tramping into obscurity' has been held over until the next issue.

John Clarkson   Roy Fenton

November 2006

Sapele Palm, German-built for Palm Line. See 'Fleet in Focus' page 133.
[Roy Fenton collection]

PALM LINE'S CARGO DESIGNS

Palm Line came into being in 1949, and over the next dozen years took delivery of several classes of cargo liner that gave its fleet a distinctive and attractive appearance. This feature showcases the 17 dry cargo ships which were built to Palm Line's own designs. As John Goble will make clear in 'Record' 36, succeeding ships – mostly from designs produced by ship builders or other owners – were less distinctive, although in some respects represented a long-overdue updating of facilities.

The pre-history of Palm Line

Towards the end of his life Lord Leverhulme, grocer turned soap and margarine magnate, began to worry that his sources of palm oil from west Africa were not secure, and this was to lead him to make some unwise decisions. Prevented by Colonial Office policy from acquiring land in the African colonies, he instead bought some established trading companies, but was then concerned with securing transport to the UK. In 1916 he purchased a fleet comprising eight relatively small steamers belonging to Herbert Watson of Manchester, which he transferred to his newly-created Bromport Steamship Co. Ltd. The timing was hardly propitious, as ship prices were rising fast thanks to mounting war losses and to the British government's failure to address merchant shipbuilding. Later in 1916 Leverhulme bought the ailing Southern Whaling and Sealing Co. Ltd., on the edge of bankruptcy due to the incompetent management and the loss of its factory ship, but with a whaling station on South Georgia. Again, the intention was to secure supplies of whale oil, but the price paid was high, and wartime conditions meant that whaling operations virtually ceased.

Ill-judged acquisitions continued when in 1920 Leverhulme bought the Niger Company, which had been granted rights by the British government to exploit the natural resources of the Niger River basin. So concerned was Leverhulme that a rival might buy the company that he acquired it in haste from which he was to repent at leisure: the Niger company was in fact close to bankruptcy. The Bromport company lost four of its eight ships during the First World War, and in 1923 – when ship prices had fallen precipitously from their post-war peak – the surviving ships were sold, inevitably at a large loss, and Leverhulme's raw materials were once again consigned to established lines such as Elder, Dempster. The Niger Company, at least, recovered from its precarious financial position, and three years after Leverhulme's death in 1928 it reversed his policy and decided to enter ship owning, probably because this was the path followed by a major rival, the African and Eastern Trade Corporation. In 1929 these two companies merged under the title United Africa Co. Ltd. (UAC Ltd.). The five-ship fleet which had come from the two constituents was enhanced, although with UAC Ltd. being outside the West African Lines Conference its ships were largely confined to loading products for Lever companies, and often sailed from Europe without cargo.

The heavy losses experienced by United Africa and the established lines during the Second World War, combined with a post-war expansion of trade, altered the nature of the West African shipping business. It was now decided that United Africa Co. Ltd. would be better operating as a common carrier, no longer confined to carrying the products of Unilever, as its parent had become. In 1949 its ships were transferred to Palm Line Ltd., a company formed by renaming the Southern Whaling and Sealing Co. Ltd. which had been dormant since Unilever withdrew from whaling in 1940. Prior agreement had been obtained with Elder, Dempster, Guinea Gulf Line and Holland West Africa Line on entering the West African Lines Conference, and Palm Line Ltd. was admitted on 1st January 1950.

Palm Line Ltd. took over 15 ocean-going ships from United Africa, comprising three motor ships and four steamers built pre-war, three steamers built during the Second World War, and five post-war steamers. Although its fleet was not particularly old, Palm Line began an ambitious new building programme, correctly predicting that the West African trade was to expand rapidly.

Nigerian (3) of 1948, the last ship built for United Africa Co. Ltd., became Palm line's *Niger Palm*. *[Ships in Focus]*

Wear and Weser

The first vessels ordered by the newly-constituted Palm Line were conventional motor ships from the Wear. They differed from pre-war United Africa ships (and indeed from the post-war *Nigerian*) in having three holds ahead of the bridge, rather than having number 3 hold between the bridge and the funnel. However, inspection of the accompanying plans reveals that in this position there were two small hatches and two derricks, serving a deep tank and various provision stores in the 'tween decks. This arrangement – a throwback to the bunker hatches on coal-burning steamers – seems to have died hard in the British merchant fleet, and *Burutu Palm* and *Africa Palm* were by no means the last British motor ships to adopt it.

Of the six holds, one was arranged to carry 1,000 tons of palm oil. Number 1 hold had an orlop deck worked into it, essentially producing a lower deck. Derrick capacity ranged from three tons to fifty tons, the latter being rigged on the foremast. Cargo-handling gear was clearly inadequate, and both ships were later fitted with two extra pairs of kingposts.

Delivery from Sunderland was late: Short Brothers blamed their steel suppliers, and claimed that they had received only five sixths of the steel allocated to the yard. Whether or not the Palm Line management accepted this explanation, they were not to use Wearside yards again for 25 years. Instead Palm was to build up a close relationship with a Tyneside yard, but first came a rather surprising further delivery.

Short Brothers Ltd., Pallion, Sunderland; 451. 8 (433.2 b.p.) x 57.8 x 23.5 feet (depth 37.2)
North Eastern-Doxford type 4-cyl. 2SCSA oil engine by North Eastern Marine Engineering Co. (1938) Ltd., Wallsend-on-Tyne; 3,000 BHP

Name	Yd no.	Launch	Trials	GT	Sold
Burutu Palm	511	23.4.1952	28.10.1952	5,410	1967
Africa Palm	512	22.7.1952	29.12.1952	5,415	1972

Burutu Palm as built (above) in the Thames in 1955, and with the extra pair of kingposts added immediately ahead and abaft of the superstructure (right). Sold in 1967, she was renamed *Tyhi* and in 1973 became *Globe Star*, but her career under this name was brief. A stranding off Mombasa on 27th April 1973 led to her being declared a constructive total loss. *[Both: Roy Fenton collection]*

A fine stern view of *Africa Palm* after fitting extra kingposts. She lasted longer than her sister, not being sold until 1972 when she became *Savoydean*. But like her sister she was to become a constructive total loss, in her case following a fire at Calcutta on 27th April 1975. *[Len Sawyer]*

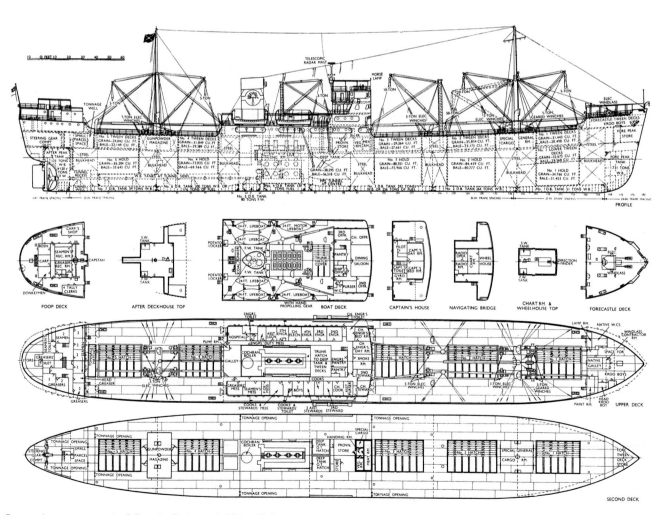

General arrangement of *Burutu Palm* and *Africa Palm*.

United Africa had built extensively in Germany before the Second World War. The parent company, Unilever, had generated considerable trading profits in the country, but was not allowed to repatriate these so chose the option of building ships in Germany instead. In 1936 and 1937 eight ocean-going motor ships came from yards at Hamburg and Bremerhaven. Although the situation was very different in post-war years, Palm maintained the relationship with German builders, initially ordering one vessel from Bremerhaven which was to be registered in the name of its German subsidiary, Olhandel und Transport GmbH of Hamburg. Surprisingly, *Sapele Palm* was a steamer, the first built for the company or its predecessor for some years, although war-built steamers had been bought and chartered. In layout, the Weser-built *Sapele Palm* was not dissimilar to her near-contemporaries from the Wear, although some of her features were distinctively German, especially the ventilator tops to the kingposts (of which she was built with two extra sets compared to *Burutu Palm*). Hull colour was initially black rather than grey, and without the white forecastles and poop which contributed to the smart appearance of the British-flag ships. *Sapele Palm* made her maiden voyage from Bremen, calling at Hamburg,

Rotterdam and Antwerp before steaming out to the West Coast of Africa. She was transferred to the British flag in 1960 and - probably because of her machinery - had a relatively short career.

A.G. Weser, Werk Seebecke, Bremerhaven; 431.1 x 57.7 x 22.7 feet
T. 3-cyl. by A.G. Weser, Werk Seebecke, Bremerhaven

Name	Yd no.	Launch	Trials	GT	Sold
Sapele Palm	744	31.7.1953	-	4,981	1966

Sapele Palm in later life, with Palm Line's grey hull but with some of the former black colour showing. Note the awning on the forecastle. She was sold in 1966, and as *Capetan Georgis* lasted until 1970 when broken up in Istanbul. *[Roy Fenton collection/Ships in Focus]*

Enter Swans

When in 1954 Palm Line was again in the market for ships, they asked for quotations from Swan, Hunter who had previously built only tankers for the company. The result was to be a fruitful relationship with the Tyneside yard which produced 12 out of the next 14 Palm Line cargo liners.

Together, Swans and Palm Line produced a radically different design. A long forecastle produced an extra 'tween deck above number 1 hold, and indeed the 'tween decks were described as especially high. There was just one mast, which carried a 75-ton heavy lift derrick, and the deck in the vicinity was strengthened for heavy cargoes. A further reflection of the variety of cargoes carried were the powder magazine between number 4 and 5 'tween decks, a deep tank amidships for palm oil, and facilities for carrying refrigerated cargo in the amidships 'tween decks. Her holds were suitable for

carrying logs. A quite steeply-raked bow completed the impression of a powerful vessel, and *Bamenda Palm*'s service speed of 13.75 knots was well exceeded on trials. There was at last a composite superstructure, although accommodation for some of the crew was still provided in the poop. The large forecastle housed the Kroomen carried to work the cargo on the West African coast.

Swan, Hunter and Wigham Richardson Ltd., Wallsend-on-Tyne; 446.7 (415 b.p.) x 58.3 x 23.4 feet
Doxford-type 4-cyl.2SCSA oil engine by Swan, Hunter and Wigham Richardson Ltd., Walker; 4,500 BHP, 13.75 knots.

Name	Yd no.	Launch	Trials	GT	Sold
Bamenda Palm	1926	14.12.1955	28.3.1956	5,042	1972
Badagry Palm	1928	11.6.1956	9.10.1956	5,042	1972

Top: *Bamenda Palm*.
Sold in 1972, subsequent
names were *Lenio, Elsa
S.K.* in 1978 and *Eternal
Sea* also in 1978. She
was broken up in
Pakistan during 1983.
[Roy Fenton collection]
Middle: *Badagry Palm* in
June 1962 on the Thames,
with a heavy lift stowed
on her fore deck. In 1972
she became *Irene's
Grace* and was broken up
in Taiwan during 1983.
[Ships in Focus]
Right: *Irene's Grace*, the
former *Badagry Palm*
leaving the Mersey in
1972. *[J. and M.
Clarkson]*

Swan's next delivery, *Elmina Palm*, was essentially a slightly enlarged version of *Bamenda Palm*, but was notable in being the first British ship with superstructure and certain fittings made of aluminium. Use of this metal was becoming established practice in passenger ships to save weight and lower the centre of gravity, but in cargo ships was not usually economical given the much greater cost of aluminium over steel. However, for Palm Line, increasing deadweight but not the draft was an important consideration, given the shallow creeks up which their ships habitually loaded. Over 74 tons was saved by reducing the weight of the superstructure, boat and poop deck awnings, some hatch covers and other parts in *Elmina Palm*.

The external differences between *Elmina Palm* and *Bamenda Palm* were subtle. The funnel was fitted on a casing that incorporated the wheelhouse and the heavy-lift derrick was of just 40-tons capacity compared with its predecessor's 75-tons. A fourth ship to this design, *Enugu Palm* entered service over a year later, and again incorporated the aluminium fittings which were to become standard for future Palm Line ships. Oddly, *Elmina* Palm did not have deep tanks for carrying vegetable oils, the only ship in the fleet not so equipped.

Swan, Hunter and Wigham Richardson Ltd., Wallsend-on-Tyne;
454.9 (425.0 b.p) x 60.3 x 23.5 feet
Doxford-type 4-cyl.2SCSA oil engine by Swan, Hunter and Wigham Richardson Ltd., Walker; 4,500 BHP, 13.5 knots.

Name	Yd no.	Launch	Trials	GT	Sold
Elmina Palm	1932	17.12.1956	11.4.1957	5,356	1977
Enugu Palm	1948	19.2.1958	24.6.1958	5,328	1978

Above: *Elmina Palm* sails from the Thames in 1957. In 1977 she became *Cyprus Sky*, in 1978 *Eastern Sky* and in 1978 *European Liberty*. She was broken up in Turkey in 1981. *[Ships in Focus]*
Right: A feature distinguishing *Enugu Palm* from her sister *Elmina Palm* was that the heavy-lift derrick was rigged ahead of the foremast, rather than abaft. This view of her entering the Tyne shows the casing on which her funnel was mounted. Names following her sale in 1978 were *Athari* and from 1979 *Seepayal*. In 1982 she was broken up in Pakistan. *[Roy Fenton collection]*

Enugu Palm. Note the aluminium awnings, especially over the poop.   *[J. and M. Clarkson collection]*

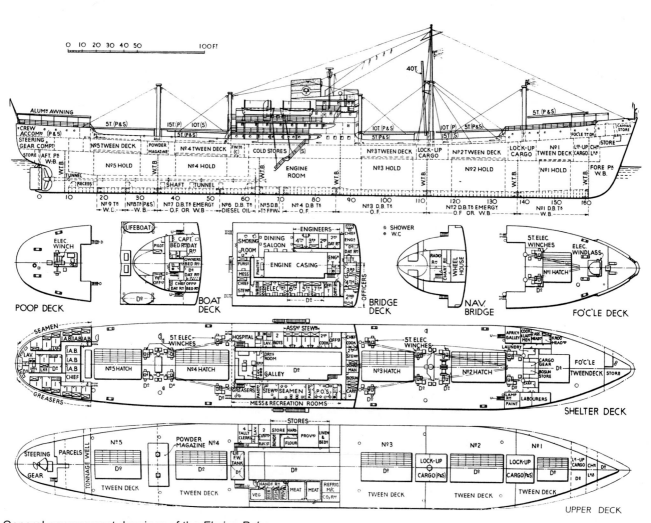

General arrangement drawings of the *Elmina Palm*.

Enlargement

Katsina Palm and *Kano Palm* were the fourth and fifth ships delivered to Palm Line by Swan, Hunter, and with the *Enugu Palm* (which was the sixth), meant that during September 1957 all three of Swan, Hunters' berths held Palm Line ships. Between the first two, Palm Line had taken delivery of its first post-war German motor ship, *Andoni Palm*, and on completion of *Kano Palm* the line's chairman could contrast the time of 44 weeks from her keel-laying to launch with that of the German yard, who achieved this in just 22 weeks. Swan, Hunter's chairman did not defend his record, but predicted that Palm Line would be surprised by the yard's next performance.

The two Ks were essentially an enlarged version of *Elmina Palm*, with deadweight increased from 7,900 to 11,200 tons. They were the largest cargo liners serving West Africa, and their owners accepted that their increased draft precluded loading at many creek ports. To supply the extra power needed, the Doxford engine had an additional cylinder.

Swan, Hunter and Wigham Richardson Ltd., Wallsend-on-Tyne; 494.9 (469 b.p) x 62.9 x 26.6 feet
Doxford-type 5-cyl. 2SCSA oil engine by Swan, Hunter and Wigham Richardson Ltd., Walker; 5,600 BHP.

Name	Yd no.	Launch	Trials	GT	Sold
Katsina Palm	1938	26.8.1957	4.12.1957	8,734	1978
Kano Palm	1946	22.11.1957	28.3.1958	8,723	1979

Upper: One of the few features which distinguished *Katsina Palm* from her smaller predecessors was the increased distance between the superstructure front and the kingposts just ahead of it. *[Roy Fenton collection]*

Middle: From sale in 1978 to her demolition in Shanghai during August 1984 *Katsina Palm* carried the name *New Dragon*, seen lying off her home port of Singapore in February 1983. *[Roy Kittle]*

Below: A deep-laden *Kano Palm* heads up the New Waterway in 1961 with a full deck cargo of logs from West Africa. She was sold in 1979, becoming *Purna Shanti* and within the same year *Island Trader*. Bombay breakers demolished her in 1982. *[Roy Fenton collection]*

German reversion

As if to remind Swan, Hunters that they were not the only shipbuilders on the block, Palm Line placed two orders with Bremer Vulkan at Vegesack. The German yard was not asked to produce anything innovative, and it seems very likely that they were given the plans of *Elmina Palm* and told to add a couple of feet here and there. When writing her up the 'Shipping and Shipbuilding Record' for 8th May 1958 seems to have used almost exactly the same copy as it used for *Elmina Palm* a year previously.

Bremer Vulkan, Vegesack; 473.0 (434.9 b.p.) x 62.2 x 23.5 feet (depth 36.0 feet)
MAN- type 2SCSA 7-cyl. by Bremer Vulkan, Vegesack; 4, 670 BHP, 14 knots

Name	Yd no.	Launch	Trials	GT	Sold
Andoni Palm	869	19.12.1957	12.3.1958	5,802	1976
Akassa Palm	870	4.2.1958	11.4.1958	5,797	1972

Above: The treatment of *Andoni Palm*'s aluminium superstructure was subtly different from that of the slightly smaller *Elmina Palm*. She was photographed in April 1966. On her sale in 1976 she ran as *Mastro Manolis* until sale for scrap in the Far East during 1982. *[J.K. Byass]*

Middle: This photograph of *Akassa Palm* under a stormy sky shows the slightly curved stem which her German builders gave her. Names subsequent to her sale in 1972 were first *Elemma*, then *Ionian Sky* from 1977, and finally *Magdalini K* from 1981 until demolition in Pakistan during 1984. *[Roy Fenton collection]*

Bottom: *Akassa Palm* wearing the funnel colours of T. and J. Harrison whilst on charter. *[J. and M. Clarkson]*

Bipod quartet

With the next orders to Swan, Hunter came a rethink of design. Three sets of bipod masts were fitted. These required less staying and were claimed to improve stowage of timber on deck, although as the bipods had a larger 'footprint' it is difficult to see their advantage. The heavy-lift derrick was now rated at 60-tons. Of more concern to the crew were improvements to the accommodation, with air conditioning and single-berth cabins for all.

At the launch of the second ship of this series, *Ilorin Palm*, Denham Christie, managing director of Swan, Hunter's yard, was proud to announce that the time from keel laying to completion had been just 23.5 weeks. This followed a £13 million modernisation programme at the Neptune Yard which was still not complete, and even better performances were to be expected when all the new equipment installed was in operation and the personnel familiar with it. Recalling Palm Line's chairman unfavourable comparison of building times in German and British yards, Swan, Hunter's Christie produced a cake which was iced with the words 'Ilorin Palm 23½ weeks' so that Palm Line's chairman could 'eat his words'. The complete building time from *Ilorin Palm* turned out to be 42 weeks, less than the 49 weeks which *Bamenda Palm* had spent on Swan's stocks. The jollifications following her launch had

no doubt been increased by the announcement that Swan, Hunter were to build two further ships. Building times were indeed reduced further for these ships, to 22 weeks from keel laying to launch. They were, however, Swan's swan song as far as Palm Line were concerned. At the final launch there were hints from the owners of further orders to come, but it was to be many years before they were to go shopping for new ships once more. With 14 new ships (12 from Swans) in six years, Palm had a modern fleet. The uncertainties of the West African trade, with newly-independent countries like Nigeria and Ghana keen to build up their own merchant fleets, undoubtedly persuaded Palm Line to behave cautiously. Palm Line initially had a 19% holding in Nigerian National Line, but sold this to Nigeria in 1964.

Swan, Hunter and Wigham Richardson Ltd., Wallsend-on-Tyne; 460.3 (430.0 b.p.) x 62.6 x 23.5 feet (depth 36.9 feet) Doxford-type 4-cyl. 2SCSA oil engine by Swan, Hunter and Wigham Richardson Ltd., Walker; 4,500 BHP, 14 knots.

Name	Yd no.	Launch	Trials	GT	Sold
Ibadan Palm	1970	20.5.1959	28.9.1959	5,658	1978
Ilorin Palm	1972	2.9.1959	8.1.1960	5,658	1979
Ikeja Palm	1982	19.12.1960	26.4.1961	5,682	1981
Ilesha Palm	1984	28.6.1961	10.1961	5,682	1979

Above: Although in size and layout *Ibadan Palm* and her sisters were similar to their predecessors, the shorter forecastle and altogether tidier appearance of funnel and superstructure made for a more handsome ship. Photographed in September 1975, *Ibadan Palm* was sold in 1978 and became first *Hind* then from 1979 *Arunkamal*, as which she was broken up in Pakistan during 1983. Below: *Ilorin Palm* had a relatively short life after sale in 1979, but carried three different names. She was first *Diamant Captain*, and in 1982 became *Cape Blanco* and then *Sea Venture*. She was broken up at Chittagong in 1983. *[Both: Ships in Focus]*

Above: Ikeja Palm. On her 1981 sale she became *GME Palma*, which in 1982 was shortened to *Palma* shortly before her demolition in Pakistan. *[J. and M. Clarkson collection]*

Middle: Proud of their ships, Palm Line published some fine postcards. This one depicts *Ilesha Palm*. In 1979 new owners renamed her *Daphnemar* and she carried this title until demolished in Pakistan during 1984. *[Roy Fenton collection]*

Bottom: *Ilesha Palm* sailing from Swansea in November 1963. *[J. and M. Clarkson collection]*

Ilesha Palm in Nigerian National Lines colours at Liverpool on the 21st August 1976. *[J. and M. Clarkson]*

16-knot express ships

When a pair of ships was needed for the West African Express service, making round voyages from Liverpool to Lagos in just 30 days, the previous design was simply fitted with a more powerful engine to give a service speed of 16 knots. Swans surpassed themselves with delivery dates, *Lobito Palm* being launched in just 20 weeks from keel laying, and running trials after a further 14 weeks. *Lagos Palm* – which was originally to have been named *Luanda Palm* – was actually delivered one month early. Swan, Hunter management declared that

they had '…never missed a delivery date in 10 years', conveniently forgetting that *Elmina Palm* was one month late due to a strike.

Swan, Hunter and Wigham Richardson Ltd., Wallsend-on-Tyne; 473.0 (440 b.p) x 63.0 x 25.0 feet (depth 37.0 feet)
Doxford-type 6-cyl. 2SCSA oil engine by Swan, Hunter and Wigham Richardson Ltd., Walker; 7,500 BHP, 16 knots.

Name	Yd no.	Launch	Trials	GT	Sold
Lobito Palm	1978	12.5.1960	8.9.1960	6,157	1979
Lagos Palm	1980	16.3.1961	25.7.1961	6,256	1981

Above: *Lobito Palm*. The heavy-lift derrick on this class had a capacity of 50 tons. On her sale in 1979 her name was abbreviated to *Lobito Pal*. Then followed a string of renamings: to *Minoa* and then *Peruvian Trader* in 1980, to *Richmond* in 1982 and to *Eurco C.* in 1983 shortly before she was broken up at Chittagong. *[Roy Fenton collection]*
Right: The economically renamed *Lobito Pal* but retaining her Palm Line colours, at Liverpool on 17th April 1979. *[J. and M. Clarkson]*

Top and middle: *Lagos Palm* at anchor on the Thames in July 1961. The last of the 'classic' Palm Line ships, in 1981 she was renamed *Lagos Palm II* to free the name for a new ship building in Poland, but was sold later that year. *[Ships in Focus]*

Right: *City of Lobito*, confusingly the former *Lagos Palm*, aground on Cheung Chau Island, Hong Kong following a typhoon in September 1983. Although refloated she was fit only for scrap, as the condition of her hull suggests. *[Roy Fenton collection]*

Photographer in Focus
DAVID de MAUS - Part 1
Ian Farquhar

After the 1861 gold rush to Otago, New Zealand, Port Chalmers became the third largest port in Australasia after Melbourne and Sydney, and it retained this status for several years. The gold rush also saw the city of Dunedin become the largest in New Zealand, a distinction it retained until the 1880s, and a number of the major businesses established in Dunedin prior to 1900 became national leaders in later years. It was from Port Chalmers that the sailing ship *Dunedin* left for London on 15th February 1882 with the first cargo of frozen meat to leave New Zealand. That pioneering voyage gave a huge impetus to meat and dairy exports and generated economic benefits that the country still enjoys today.

Port Chalmers' shipping history is all the more richer for the efforts of David Alexander de Maus, who was established as a photographer in the port for over 50 years from the 1870s. Descended from Huguenots, he was born in Edinburgh on 8th April 1847 and came to Port Chalmers on the ship *Caribou* in 1867. He quickly learnt the photographic business from his brother James. His record of shipping at Port Chalmers has, to a large extent, survived; mainly no doubt because from the early 1870s he photographed such a range of early shipping, both sail and steam. Although New Zealand's premier archive, the Alexander Turnbull Library in Wellington, purchased the remnants of his collection in the late 1930s, many prints had already been supplied around the

world, and de Maus images are available from many sources, although the Turnbull Library has the largest set of original glass plates.

De Maus was into everything in Port Chalmers. He was elected to the Port Chalmers Borough Council in 1877 as a councillor and later had four terms as mayor, in 1899-1901, 1903-1906, 1909-1910 and 1912-1913. He was also a member of the Otago Harbour Board from 1904 to 1910. He was president or vice-president of the rowing, cricket, football and hockey clubs, as well as demonstrating his skills as a singer, and as a writer of plays, light operas and topical sketches. He toured some of the goldfields providing the miners with humour and songs in his fine tenor voice, before settling in Port Chalmers in 1869. In 1893 he became the first New Zealand resident to be prosecuted for selling a nude photograph, and was fined 3 dollars and costs.

Once regular steam services were established out of Port Chalmers, de Maus gradually built up a significant collection of shipping views and sold prints to officers and crew. He was sometimes able to build up a montage for masters and officers, with photos of all the ships in which they had served. Port Chalmers was also the headquarters of the Union Steam Ship Company of New Zealand Ltd., a company established in Dunedin in 1875, and which subsequently became the largest shipping company in the southern

NEBRASKA
Henry Steers, Greenport, New York, launched 1865 as Managua *and completed in 1867 as* Nebraska; *2,135gt, 268 x 41 x 26 feet. Vertical beam engine by Neptune Ironworks, New York; 1,500 IHP.* In 1871 the American William H. Webb gained a mail contract to operate a service from San Francisco to Auckland, Wellington, Lyttelton and Port Chalmers, with the ships connecting with a steamer from Sydney at the island of Kandavu in Fiji. Three wooden side-wheel steamers owned by the California, New Zealand and Australian Steam Navigation Company of San Francisco were employed and the second was *Nebraska,* shown berthed at Port Chalmers in March 1871. The two other paddlers were the *Nevada* and *Dacotah*, but the service could not meet the contract's demands and it finished when *Nebraska* left Auckland in April 1873. She was sold to the Pacific Mail Steamship Company in 1873, then to Goodall, Nelson and Perkins, San Francisco in 1876, and was scrapped in 1878.

hemisphere. He also painted reproductions of some of their ships and sold them as well as photographs. A very diminutive figure, de Maus was well liked in Port Chalmers and in later years he had to live with the name 'Daddy' which was derived from his initials. He died on 17th July 1925 and his widow then joined the rest of her family in England, taking a consignment of glass plates with her. One of de Maus's daughters married Captain E.T. Grayson, a Shaw, Savill and Albion master. Katy Matheson carried on the photographic

business until about 1948 when it closed and she moved to Wanganui. Many of the photographic plates of people and events in Port Chalmers were destroyed but the impersonal plates of the ships were retained as they represented the best source of income from the business.

The coverage of pre-1900 shipping in photographs taken by de Maus ranks with that of the Gould family of Greenwich and William Livermore in Sydney. All the images used in this article have come from the author's collection.

MONGOL (right)
Howden and Co., Glasgow, 1873;
2,265gt, 300 x 35 x 31.6 feet
Compound direct acting by Howden
and Co., Glasgow.
When the W.H. Webb service collapsed, the Australian and American Steamship Company was established, with subsidies from the governments of New Zealand and New South Wales, Australia. The steamer *Mongol* entered the new service by being positioned on her maiden voyage from Plymouth to Port Chalmers, arriving at the latter port in February 1874 after a passage of 51 days 18 hours, of which 29 days were under steam. She was owned by the New York, London and China Steam Ship Co. Ltd., London and came out under charter to the New Zealand Shipping Company. The photograph shows the ship at the Quarantine Anchorage, Port Chalmers as during the voyage there had been outbreaks of measles, scarlet fever and bronchitis which caused 16 deaths. She sailed from Port Chalmers on 22nd February to enter the new mail service but only made one voyage across the Pacific, being wrecked on 12th December 1874 about one mile east of South Ninepin Island, 14 miles from Hong Kong,

whilst on passage from Hong Kong to Yokohama. A total of 17 lives were lost.

CITY OF SAN FRANCISCO (below)
J. Roach and Son, Chester,
Pennsylvania, 1875; 3,009gt, 339 x
40.2 x 27.5 feet
Compound engine
At the end of 1874 the Pacific Mail Steamship Company of San Francisco announced plans for a new ten-year mail contract from San Francisco to Australia and New Zealand. For the first year of the contract a New Zealand coastal service was provided with calls at Auckland, Napier,

Wellington, Lyttelton and Port Chalmers but this was discontinued at the end of 1876 in favour of the vessels calling only at Auckland. The *City of San Francisco* is shown at anchor off Port Chalmers on 8th December 1875. She made one further call at Port Chalmers before the service was rationalised on Auckland, but it remained in place for the full ten years. *City of San Francisco* was built for the Pacific Mail Steamship Company and was wrecked on an uncharted rock on Tartar Shoal off Punta Maldonado, Mexico on 16th May 1877 while on a voyage Panama to San Francisco.

CITY OF NEW YORK

J. Roach and Son, Chester, Pennsylvania, 1875; 3,019gt, 339.0 x 40.2 x 20.5 feet Compound engine

A sister of the *City of San Francisco*, the *City of New York* arrived at Port Chalmers on 10th November 1875 and made two further calls at the port in 1876. Auckland became the only port of call in New Zealand. On her first round voyage it was reported that the *City of New York* had traveled 18,141 miles with 66 days at sea. Also owned by Pacific Mail Steamship Company, she became a total loss when she struck Point Bonita in San Francisco Bay when outward bound for China on 26th October 1893.

GRANADA

Harlan and Hollingsworth, Wilmington, Delaware, 1873; 2,572gt, 280 x 40 x 20 feet Compound surface condensing engine by John Elder and Co., Glasgow.

Another vessel of the Pacific Mail Steamship Company, the *Granada* is shown at Port Chalmers in March 1876. She remained in service with Pacific Mail until she was wrecked on Point Tejupan, about 40 miles south south east of Manzanillo, Mexico on 22nd June 1889 whilst on passage San Francisco to Panama.

COLIMA

J. Roach and Sons, Chester, Pennsylvania, 1873; 2,905gt, 299.7 x 39.8 x 20.3 feet Compound engine.

A slightly larger steamer than *Granada*, the Pacific Mail's *Colima* lost her propeller off Akaroa, Banks Peninsula, New Zealand in April 1876 and had to return to Port Chalmers for dry-docking, so that a new propeller could be fitted. The photo shows *Colima* in dock at Port Chalmers on 20th April 1876. Built for Pacific Mail, she remained with the company until 27th May 1895 when she capsized and foundered following a boiler explosion 50 miles south of Manzanillo, Mexico, while on passage San Francisco to Panama. 160 lives were lost.

ZEALANDIA (right)
John Elder and Company, Glasgow, 1875; 2,730gt, 377.0 x 37.4 x 18.6 feet Compound inverted engine by John Elder and Company, Glasgow
The Pacific Mail Steamship Company's contract for the Australasian service stipulated that one ship must be in Sydney at all times, and in order to maintain the schedule four steamers were needed for the service. The company chartered two newly built British vessels, the first, *Zealandia,* was closely followed by her sister *Australia.* The photograph shows *Zealandia* at Port Chalmers on 23rd August 1876. The charter was taken over by the Oceanic Steamship Company of San Francisco in 1890 and the vessel purchased by that company, being under Hawaiian registry from 1890 to 1898 and United States registry from 1898 to 1917. *Zealandia* was employed as a military transport from 1898 to 1902, being later sold to Charles L. Dimon, then the Fisk Trading Company, both of New York. Her final owner in 1916 was the Universal Transportation Company of New York. On passage New York to Liverpool she ran aground on Horse Bank, three miles west of Southport, Lancashire on 3rd April 1917. Under heavy swells the vessel broke in two and quickly became a total loss. Another photograph of her appeared on page 260 in 'Record' 32.

STAR OF THE EAST (middle)
Charles Connell and Company, Glasgow, 1876; 757gt, 183.3 x 30.7 x 18.5 feet
Many of the de Maus photographs of sailing ships were taken while they lay under the cliff at Export Pier, Port Chalmers and the background is familiar in a wide range of images featured in many published books. Today the cliff seen behind the *Star of the East* has been cut back to the position of her foremast, in order to provide more storage areas for logs and container facilities. The iron barque *Star of the East* owned by Sir R.W. Cameron, London came to Port Chalmers with general cargo from New York in August 1888.

DUNEDIN (bottom)
R. Duncan and Co., Port Glasgow, 1874; 1,320gt, 241.0 x 36.1 x 20.9 feet
The photograph of the sailing ship *Dunedin* shown here has been widely reproduced because of the vessel's distinction as the first ship to carry frozen meat from New Zealand in 1882 – an event that dramatically changed the economic fortunes of the country. Often the caption states it shows the vessel loading the first cargo of meat, but the photograph (showing smoke coming from the refrigerating machinery) was

taken at least nine months later when Shaw, Savill and Company of London and the Albion Line of Glasgow had merged to form the Shaw, Savill and Albion. This company's vessels were grey-hulled with white-painted ports, compared to the Albion Line colours of black hull and red boot-topping. Many artists have used this image as their model when recording the epic voyage in the various frozen meat anniversaries. The Frank H. Mason paintings for the 50th anniversary in 1932 and again for the 75th in 1957 shows the *Dunedin* in Shaw, Savill and Albion colours. The

colour scheme was also used in 1957 by New Zealand artist Howard Mallitte and for a special painting by Kevin Tweddell which was widely used for the centennial celebrations in 1982. It will likely be a difficult task to introduce the correct colours of the ship after over 75 years of it being wrongly portrayed! At least in all the errant paintings the artists have shown an Albion Line house flag flying at the masthead. *Dunedin* made 17 outward passages to New Zealand (12 to Port Chalmers) and was lost when she went missing on her return to London in 1890.

BRAHMIN (above)
R. Steele and Co., Greenock, 1876;
1,325gt, 231.4 x 36.3 x 21.9 feet
The smart-looking iron barque
Brahmin is shown at Port Chalmers in
December 1890 having completed an
85-day passage at the end of a New
Zealand Shipping Company charter.
Owned by J. and W. Stewart of
Greenock, the ship made four voyages
to New Zealand with migrants, but only
one to Port Chalmers. All the voyages
were under charter to the New
Zealand Shipping Company. She was
sold to Ant. Dom. Bordes et fils of
Dunkirk in 1893 and renamed *Quillota*,
remaining with that company until she

was wrecked off Sunderland on 3rd
November 1901 whilst on passage
from Nantes to the Tyne.

VICTORY (below)
Richardson, Duck and Co., Stockton-
on-Tees, 1882; 2,848gt, 324.0 x 38.2 x
25.5 feet
C.2-cyl. by Blair and Co. Ltd.,
Stockton-on-Tees
Prior to the advent of permanent
steamers in the trade between London
and New Zealand, both the New
Zealand Shipping Company and Shaw,
Savill and Albion Company chartered
steamers fitted with refrigerated
chambers. One of these early

steamers, the *Victory,* is shown
anchored off Port Chalmers in
December 1883, after a 57-day
passage from London. She was
chartered by Shaw, Savill and Albion
from her owners, McIntyre Brothers
and Company of Newcastle, and made
two further voyages to New Zealand in
1884. *Victory* was sold to A. Mancini
of Genoa in 1896 and renamed
Costanza. She retained this name
when sold to C. Ruchat & Company of
Livorno in 1901 and was wrecked on
McCammon's Rock, near Cloughey,
County Down on 22nd December 1905
on passage from Buenos Aires to
Belfast with a cargo of maize.

FLORIDA (above)
Charles Mitchell and Co., Newcastle-upon-Tyne, 1882; 3,138gt, 336.6 x 41.2 x 26.5 feet
C. 2-cyl. by North Eastern Marine Engineering Co. Ltd., Sunderland
Another Shaw, Savill and Albion Company charter was the two-funnelled *Florida*, photographed at Port Chalmers on 30th March 1884 after a passage of 53 days 18 hours from London. She was chartered for a second voyage and her sister ship *Bombay* was also chartered for voyages to New Zealand. Both vessels were owned by Nelson, Donkin and Company of London. Fitted with refrigeration for the carriage of frozen meat, the major portion of her first cargo had to be condemned although there were no problems with the quality on the second voyage. She was sold to C. Christensen of Sandefjord in 1908 and renamed *Orn* under the Norwegian flag. Five years later ownership passed to R. Fredriksen of Christiana and she became the *Falkland*. She stranded at Santa Maria, Uruguay on 13th November 1913 while on passage from Tonsberg to South Georgia to rendezvous with the whaling fleet.

SORRENTO (lower)
A. Stephen and Sons, Glasgow, 1881; 2,371gt, 320.0 x 36.2 x 24.6 feet
C. 2-cyl. by A. Stephen and Sons, Glasgow

Robert Sloman of Hamburg had been sending ships to Australia from 1873 and from 1881 the company developed a permanent steamer service. Some of his vessels were fitted for the carriage of frozen meat and, following the successful voyage of the Albion Line sailing ship *Dunedin* which left Port Chalmers on 15th February 1882, Sloman decided to send two steamers to New Zealand to load cargoes of frozen meat. The first, *Marsala,* was the first steamer to load meat in New Zealand but her refrigerating machinery broke down on the voyage and her cargo was ruined. The second vessel was the *Sorrento* and she arrived Port Chalmers on 18th November 1882 and sailed for London on 7th December. No further Sloman vessels crossed to New Zealand to load, and all other frozen meat was lifted by Britsh shipping companies. *Sorrento* remained in the Sloman fleet until 10th November 1902 when she stranded at Minarton near Muros, Spain, while on passage Messina to Hamburg, and became a total loss.

IONIC (above)
Harland and Wolff, Belfast, 1883;
4,753gt, 439.4 x 44.2 x31.5 feet
C.4-cyl. by Harland and Wolff, Belfast
1894: Q.4-cyl. by Harland and Wolff, Belfast

Although White Star Line vessels of the Oceanic Steam Navigation Co. Ltd., Liverpool shared the Shaw, Savill and Albion berth from 1885, the first White Star Line steamer to New Zealand was the *Ionic,* which was chartered by the New Zealand Shipping Company. On her first voyage for this company she made a record passage of 43 days, 22 hours from London to Wellington, averaging 12.5 knots on a coal consumption of 45 tons per day. When she arrived at Wellington on 11th June 1883 she was the largest and longest steamer to come to New Zealand. She saw service as a transport during the Boer War and in 1900 she was sold to George Thompson's Aberdeen Line and renamed *Sophocles.* She was sold for scrap in 1908 and demolished at Morecambe in April. The photograph shows her at Port Chalmers with the taller funnel which was fitted during an extensive refit when she was re-engined in 1894. Originally she carried yards for sails on all four masts but following the refit in 1894 these were confined to the foremast.

COPTIC (below)
Harland and Wolff, Belfast, 1881;
4,448gt, 430.2 x 42.2 x 24.4 feet
Q.4-cyl. by John Jack and Co., Liverpool
1894: T. 3-cyl. by Harland and Wolff, Belfast

Coptic entered the New Zealand trade in 1884 in the joint service provided by Shaw, Savill and Albion Company and the Oceanic Steam Navigation Company. She made her first visit to Port Chalmers on 14th July 1884 after a 47-day passage from Plymouth via Hobart. The photo shows the shorter funnel with which the ship was originally fitted. She remained in the New Zealand trade until 1894. *Coptic* was sold to the Pacific Mail Steamship Company of San Francisco in 1906 and renamed *Persia* the following year. In 1916 ownership passed to the Toyo Kisen K.K., Yokohama and she became the *Persia Maru*, being laid up from 1924 and scrapped at Osaka in 1926.

KENT (above)
*Hawthorn, Leslie and Co. Ltd.,
Newcastle-upon-Tyne, 1899; 5,464gt,
420.0 x 54.0 x 28.6 feet*
*T. 3-cyl by Hawthorn, Leslie and Co.
Ltd., Newcastle-upon-Tyne*
The spartan lines of the cargo ship *Kent*
are apparent in this broadside view.
Although completed in 1899 it was not
until September 1902 that she made her
first call at Port Chalmers. The first of
six sister ships ordered by the Federal
Steam Navigation Company, *Kent* was
sold to Vestey Brothers in 1915 and
remained within the Blue Star Line
group until she was broken up in 1934.

LUNA (below)
*Greenwich, Kent, 1864; 311gt, 170.1 x
24.0 x 8.5 feet*
Double oscillating engines, 120 NHP
Built as a fast paddle steamer, *Luna*
made two successful round trip runs
from Havana to Galveston as a
blockade runner during the American
Civil War. She then returned to
London and came out to Australia
1868-1870, after which she was sold
to the Government of New Zealand as
a lighthouse tender but also served to
transport the Governor General to
official gatherings around New
Zealand. She is shown on one of her

visits to Port Chalmers in 1872 when
the Governor opened the Graving
Dock on 15th March and then on 31st
December when the railway link
between Port Chalmers and Dunedin
was opened. She could make up to
17 knots but was heavy on coal and in
1877 she was sold to Martin Kennedy
of Greymouth and then in 1894 to the
Westport Coal Company of Dunedin,
with most of her time from 1877 being
employed as a coal hulk. She was
condemned and blown up in
spectacular fashion at a Lyttelton
Regatta day on 24th January 1903.

SAMSON *James Paterson, Glasgow, 1854; 181gt, 150.0 x 17.6 x 8.3 feet   Oscillating engine, 80 NHP*

Amid a forest of sailing ship masts at the Railway Wharf, Port Chalmers in 1873 lies the small paddle steamer *Samson*. She played an important role with a number of prominent shipping companies in Australasia. She was carried out to Sydney in parts for the Australasian Steam Navigation Company and was rebuilt at the company's works at Pyrmont. *Samson* was sold to the Gippsland Steam Navigation Company in 1866 and crossed the Tasman Sea to New Zealand in 1871. Briefly owned by John Macfarlane of Auckland she then came to Port Chalmers under the Harbour Steam Company, managed by James Mills who founded the Union Steamship Company of New Zealand in 1875. *Samson* remained under Mills' ownership until 1878 when she was sold to the West Wanganui Coal Company at Wanganui. It was under this ownership that she stranded in the Waitara River on 23rd July 1881 and became a total loss. Originally 120-feet long she was lengthened in 1860 to 150 feet and over her 27 years of service she proved a very lucky and reliable performer.

(To be continued)

151

J. WHARTON (SHIPPING) LTD. Part 1
Ken Garrett

Early days

Joseph Wharton was born of a farming family at Winterton in 1860. At the age of fourteen he escaped from the grindingly hard life on a Lincolnshire farm and ran away to sea. His new life could barely have been much easier but with its wider horizons it attracted an energetic youngster. In February 1884 Joseph Wharton married Sarah, the daughter of Charles Turgoose, mariner of Drypool, and the ceremony took place in the parish church of St. Peter, Drypool.

He must have done well in his chosen profession because, in April 1885, Joseph was appointed master of the ketch *Try On* at Goole. The ketch was owned by Israel Jackson of Goole and was one of many sailing craft engaged on the coal trade from the Humber to the Thames. Three years later, in 1888, Joseph purchased 16 of the vessel's 64 shares, the transaction was recorded by the Registrar of Ships at Goole who also noted that the purchaser described himself as a ship owner and resident at Keadby.

Captain Wharton was relieved by Harvey Woodward at Newcastle in April 1890 and he came ashore to set up his own business as a coal merchant at Keadby and at neighbouring Althorpe. Coal from Derbyshire and South Yorkshire had come to Keadby in barges along the Stainforth and Keadby Canal since it opened in 1802, but from 1860 the coal had also arrived by rail to be tipped into larger barges and towed elsewhere. Originally Joseph Wharton's business was to sell domestic coal from his pony and dray around the local villages, but soon he also became the Keadby agent for the Humber Steam Towing Co-operative Society Ltd. Their tugs towed coal-laden barges from the canal to destinations along the River Trent and beyond. His business gradually expanded from a little wooden office, thanks to contacts he had made during his seafaring days with the South Yorkshire pits, ship and barge owners, agents and coal factors.

Keadby, with a population of a little over 500, already had a wharf for the shipment of coal and other goods. For such a small place it had excellent communications and was not only served by the Manchester, Sheffield and Lincolnshire Railway and the Keadby and Stainforth Canal but also the

Joseph Wharton 'cross braced with watch chain' from a painting by Roy Reynolds.
[Company archives]

Gainsborough United Steam Packet steamers called there every day on their trip from Hull to Gainsborough. A proper jetty for passengers using the steamers was erected about 1890 by Thomas Coggan, a prominent local landowner. The river was a most important feature of local life and much of the adjacent farmland had been enriched by the warping process. This involved a technique of controlled flooding of the land by the muddy river water and later draining away the surplus water after the rich alluvial sediment had been deposited.

Wharton's business prospered steadily with shipments increasing and the destinations becoming further and further beyond the Humber area to London and the south coast. The shares in the *Try On* were sold back to Israel Jackson in 1897. He died in 1905 but the ketch remained in sail under her new owner until 1907 when she sank off the Gunfleet Beacon in the Thames estuary while on passage from New Holland to London with house coal. Happily, Captain Craven and all his crew were saved.

Canals and railways

At this point in the narrative it is appropriate to outline the development of the local canals and railways that had such an important influence on the company's affairs. The Stainforth and Keadby Canal was authorised by an Act of Parliament in 1793 and extended by Acts of 1798 and 1809. When the Canal opened in 1802 Keadby was given a new importance and became a stopping place for the Hull and Gainsborough steam packet services. The River Don Navigation had been incorporated in 1726 and, following an unsuccessful attempt to purchase it in 1837, leased the canal in 1849 in what was probably a tidying up operation before the canals were merged with the South Yorkshire, Doncaster and Goole Railway in 1850. The combined company was called the South Yorkshire Railway and River Don Co. Ltd. One of the objectives was to bring coal along the canal from the collieries for shipment at Keadby. Coal shipments were already taking place from the canal and a study by the Hull port authorities conducted in 1849 showed that coal from the area was being taken as far afield as London, Lynn, Wisbech, Spalding, Lowestoft, Saltfleet and Downham.

The merger seems to have had little effect at first but in 1859 a railway line was laid alongside the canal between Thorne and Keadby and the first train load of coal for shipment arrived at Keadby in February of the following year, 1860. Coal could now be loaded directly into ships alongside the new riverside staith at what was to become known as Railway Wharf. Extra sidings and staiths were built alongside the canal at various times between 1871 and 1886 to accommodate increased barge traffic. Competition was fierce and in 1870 the canal dues were reduced by three pence per ton in answer to a similar reduction on the Aire and Calder Canal whose great advantage was direct access into Goole docks.

In 1864 the South Yorkshire Railway and River Don Company was taken over by the Manchester, Sheffield and Lincolnshire Railway which, in a grandiose rationalisation, changed its name to the Great Central Railway to coincide with the opening of its London extension into Marylebone Station in 1897.

The original riverside staith had its limitations and it was replaced with a new steam powered ramped staith in 1912. Sam Fay had become the general manager of the Great Central Railway in 1903 and it is thought that he was persuaded to build the new staith after discussions with Joseph Wharton. He was knighted when the King opened the new Immingham Docks in 1912 and remained the general manager until the railway grouping of 1923. The staith remained in operation until closed by British Rail in the late 1960s. Railway Wharf remains, hard by the entrance to the canal, but all connections to the railway system have been removed. It is a curious fact that the railways, with all their glamour and passion, have in some cases been outlived by the mundane and often neglected canals.

The First World War and the Trent
The First World War was a very difficult time and shipments of coal from the Humber were severely disrupted and those from the Trent slowed to a trickle because of a lack of ships. By 1917 the general situation had become sufficiently serious for a War Cabinet committee to consider the problem. They found that, before the war, coal represented about one third of all the UK's rail traffic. But in addition to the amount railborn,

23,000,000 tons were carried annually by sea to London and other centres from ports bordering the coalfields. With fewer ships available and abnormal risks at sea, this great tonnage – practically all of which had to be carried over long distances – was thrown on to the already over-pressed railways. The War Cabinet accepted the report and immediately put in hand measures to limit the movement of coal to that strictly laid down by guidelines. The effect of this was to restrict even further the amount of coal being sent by sea from the Yorkshire coalfield to the traditional markets in the south of England.

Inter-war developments
Once again the Wharton business depended on local deliveries around the neighbouring villages by pony and dray. Having lost the coal shipments, it took some years to reorganise and to get moving again after the war and things did not get back to normal until the mid-1920s. Joseph's son Jack Illingworth Wharton had been born in 1907 and educated at Thorne Grammar School where he excelled at football, and now started to work in the family business.. This was probably bound to happen sooner or later but it was accidentally pre-empted. One evening, during his apprenticeship, Jack left his girl friend's house in Kirton Lindsey to ride on his motor cycle to the nearby locomotive sheds for the night shift. He fell off into a ditch and later one of his mates patched him up using the work's first aid kit. He was later disciplined and invited to pay for the bandages because his injuries were sustained in a 'non works accident.' He reacted strongly to this injustice, left his job and went to work with Joseph, by this time a well-known Trentside character.

One of the limiting factors for ships trading to the wharves on the River Trent has always been the bar at the Trent Falls where the Trent joins the Ouse to become the Humber. In the days just after the First World War the limiting draft on spring tides was considered to be 14 feet 6 inches (4.43 metres). Ships with a draft approaching this figure would only be considered on rising spring tides so that if the ship went aground there would still be the chance of floating off at the next high water. Even so there was, and still is, the possibility of going aground when going upstream with the flood tide and being swung athwart the river. This could have dire consequences with possible danger to the ships sternframe and rudder or, even worse, a broken back.

In practical terms the twin constraints of the bar and water on the berth itself had limited the size of ships loading at Keadby to a modest deadweight of 250 tons. Jack Wharton thought this to be unnecessarily restrictive and without telling his father he fixed a larger ship of 400 tons. The ship was *Saint Enoch*, a steamer with engines aft built in 1918 for J. and A. Gardner and Co. Ltd. of Glasgow. Joseph was concerned when he learned of the plan but when the ship loaded and sailed without mishap he rewarded enterprise by officially taking Jack into the business and allowed him to handle the trade in basic slag which amounted to about 30,000 tons a year.

Railway Wharf at Keadby. The coal tip can be seen on the extreme left. *[Author's collection}*

The business expands

Saint Enoch may well have cast a lucky spell because from this point the Wharton shipbroking business seems to have gradually expanded and, although the path was never smooth, the seeds were sown for later developments. Ships were fixed for coal cargoes, not only from Keadby but also Goole to the south and south west coast ports. Cargoes of Cornish china clay would bring the ships back to Antwerp, Rotterdam or other near-continental ports where they would be ideally placed to load fertilisers back for Goole. This neat triangle made good commercial sense.

In December 1931 Jack Wharton married Gladys Cundall of Kirton Lindsey and, in later years, Gladys became very active in the business and was a director of several Wharton companies. Three years later, in August 1934, Joseph Wharton died leaving Jack, then aged 27,

Brendonia (1). *[Dave Hocquard collection]*

to carry on the business and also the title of Trent Harbour Master with jurisdiction from the Trent Falls to Gainsborough. Jack and Gladys Wharton had three children, Brenda, Elizabeth and John Steven who was born in 1943. In addition to his shipping business, Jack was involved in farming with a 200 acre farm at Brigg and later a farm at Alkborough. He was also chairman of the Keadby and District Agricultural Society for many years. Another interest was the breeding of shire horses and his favourite animal, Tommy Atkins, won many show prizes. Interest in local affairs led him to become chairman of the Axholme Rural District Council and a school governor. Neither did he neglect the arts and was for some years president of the Scunthorpe Operatic Society. He retained a great love of football and became a director of Scunthorpe United Football Club in 1947 later becoming chairman until poor health forced him to resign in 1968. He remained president of the club until he died.

As many shippers had done before him and no doubt some might do again, Jack Wharton decided to become a ship owner. One can only speculate on his real reasons but he was encouraged by his wife and their close family friendship with Charles Craggs, the chairman of Goole Shipbuilding and Repairing Co. Ltd. After giving the specification much thought and incorporating some of his own ideas, he placed an order for one of the 'Goole Proficient Motor Coasters' in 1936. He mortgaged two houses at Keadby to pay the deposit. The keel was laid on 7th November 1936 as yard number 325 and was launched by his eldest daughter Brenda, then still an infant, as *Brendonia* on Monday 15th March 1937. The ship ran trials and was handed over to the new owner on 10th July 1937. A very simple single-deck ship, she had a raised forecastle and poop, cruiser stern, teak wheelhouse, two wooden hatches serving one hold and a German Deutz main engine. She is believed to have been the

first motor coaster on the Goole Register and was certainly one of the first of such small ships to be equipped with a radio telephone.

A milestone in the development of the company came on 4th November 1938 when J. Wharton (Shipping) Ltd. was incorporated with a nominal capital of £5,000. The first directors and shareholders were Jack Wharton and John Harrison, a Scunthorpe solicitor, and they were soon joined by Gladys Wharton.

A second ship soon followed whose keel was laid on 15th February 1939. She was launched as *Gladonia* by Mrs Gladys Wharton on 20th June and handed over after successful trials on 31st July 1939. She had been fixed to carry a cargo of fish oil in drums to Hamburg but this was cancelled at the last minute because of the threat of war.

The Second World War

The reality of war soon hit the company when the *Brendonia* was run down and sunk with the loss of three lives on 11th September 1939. She had loaded a cargo of coal at Goole for Fowey and had sailed south in convoy FS 2 arriving at

Gladonia (1). *[Charles Hill]*

Brendonia (2). [J. and M. Clarkson collection]

Southend on the 10th. She then went to anchor in the Downs to await the westbound convoy OA 3 to take her down channel to her destination. During the night she was struck by the British steamer *Alderpool* (4,313/1936) and sank. Although the navy and other rescue services were on the scene very quickly, three crew members were lost in the dark.

The *Gladonia* survived the war despite being often in the thick of things. In January 1941 she was attacked by German aircraft when in convoy near the Sunk Light Vessel, inward bound to London with a cargo of coal. She received two direct hits causing considerable damage to bulwarks and deck stringers. The force of the explosions also affected the shaft alignment causing damage to the bearings. The ship was repaired at Rotherhithe and returned to service a month later.

A year later, in February 1942, *Gladonia* was attacked by two German bombers while in a North Sea convoy. Probably better prepared and armed by this time, the ship's machine gunners forced the bombers to drop their load prematurely thus missing the ship. The Chief Engineer, Rex Guy, was credited with shooting down one of the attackers. Captain Tom Cross and one of the sailors were given official commendations for their part in the action.

The *Gladonia* was twice in trouble in 1943, both incidents being unconnected with enemy action. On the first occasion, in May, she was lying alongside Flixborough Wharf when, in dense fog, she was struck by the dumb barge *Ablen* owned by the Flixborough Shipping Co. Ltd. The damage was only superficial but the point to note is that the barge came under Wharton control in later years. The second incident, in June, was more serious and the ship sustained extensive bow damage in a collision with

one of His Majesty's vessels at Ipswich where *Gladonia* had brought a cargo of coal from Blyth.

During the war the company managed two small vessels for the Ministry of War Transport. The first was the *Empire Head* built at Wallsend by Clelands in 1941. The ship was originally managed by T.E. Evans and Co. Ltd. of London who also operated some of their own 'Goole Proficient Motor Coasters'. Whartons took over the management of the ship in 1942. As managers, the company had the first option to purchase the ship when she became surplus to Ministry requirements and duly bought her for £12,000 in September 1945. She was renamed *Brendonia* to replace the ship lost early in the war.

The second ship was the *Empire Farouche* which was built at Goole and entered service in October 1944. She was one of a large class of prefabricated ships using simple straight-line construction methods and destined to assist with the invasion of Europe. The ships were designed to be able to

Lizzonia in dry dock at Goole. [J. and M. Clarkson]

155

run straight onto the beaches and remain there, upright and aground, until the next high water. The class were originally ordered as tankers and were given the name CHANT (Channel Tanker) followed by a number. As things turned out, the need for tankers was not as great as had been expected and some of the class were completed as dry cargo ships. This ship was originally ordered as *Chant 35* and when changed to a dry cargo ship became *Fabric 35* but finally the Ministry relented and gave the dry cargo ships proper *Empire-* names. She was managed by Whartons from the outset and was purchased by the company for £8,000 in the fourth allocation of surplus tonnage in July 1946. She was renamed *Lizzonia* after Jack Wharton's youngest daughter Elizabeth Angela, born in 1941.

Lizzonia (1). [Charles Hill]

After a number of mechanical problems the Blackstone main engine of *Lizzonia* was changed in 1956 for a similar but slightly more powerful unit made by the same engine builder. By this time the Blackstone company had been taken over by Lister and in recording the change it appears that the registrar confused the provenance because the documents probably came from R.A. Lister (Marine Sales) Ltd. The ship was still not without her problems but none so obvious as when she sank alongside while discharging coal at Teignmouth in November 1948. It was simply a matter of a sea inlet valve having been left open. This occurred on a Friday

Stevonia (1). [Charles Hill]

night and yet she was pumped out, dried out and sailed on Monday for Par to load china clay for Antwerp. Her end came in 1961 when she was in collision with the Swedish vessel *Arctic Ocean* (4,029/1948) in dense fog three miles from the Varne Light Vessel while on passage from Antwerp to Plymouth with a cargo of potash. Luckily, Captain Thomas and all his crew were picked up by the Swedish vessel and taken to Malmo for repatriation.

Post-war rebuilding

The company survived the war with the *Gladonia* and the two managed ships and soon began to think about new tonnage. After some discussions it was decided to return to Goole for the first post-war newbuilding and as yard number 467 the ship was laid down in January 1947. She was launched as *Stevonia* after Jack Wharton's son Steven, born in 1943. The ship was a slightly larger version of the pre-war *Gladonia* and came into service in January 1948. It is interesting to note that unlike her earlier sisters she had a British Polar main engine and not one of the German Deutz engines that so dominated the pre-war market.

Another product of the Goole yard came into the company with the purchase of the *Dron* in 1950. She had been built as the *Conida* in 1936 and was one of the larger versions of the Goole standard design. The fleet now numbered five vessels, all registered in Goole. The new purchase was renamed *Jackonia*

thus completing the family circle and served the company well until sold to Irish owners for further trading in 1963.

A further addition came in 1954 when the company purchased the Dutch-built and owned *Oceaan*. Immediate family names had been used up and, widening the scope just a little, the ship was renamed *Tryonia* in memory of Joseph Wharton's command *Try On*. The work required to register the ship under the British flag was carried out at Greenhithe. British shipowners had long felt aggrieved by the alterations

The *Dron* at Falmouth 2nd March 1949. The following year she was bought by J. Wharton (Shipping) Ltd. and renamed *Jackonia.* *[J. and M. Clarkson collection]*

Tryonia in the River Ouse after her foremast had been removed and a shorter mast stepped forward to carry her navigation lights. *[Charles Hill]*

required when they tried to put a foreign ship under the British flag. Some of the alterations have been substantial and others quite trivial but they have all cost money and some have made a mockery of the international nature of the Safety of Life at Sea and other conventions. Although the requirements have become more lenient of late, many owners still opt for one of the free flags rather than face the risks of incurring unnecessary costs.

The ship's trading patterns in these early post-war years were much the same as those developed before the war: coal to the south and south west ports followed by china clay or roadstone back to the Thames or near continent with cargoes of potash, grain or fertilisers to get back into position to load more coal.

The *Stevonia* had a problem when her cargo of wheat shifted in very bad weather on a voyage from London to Newcastle in January 1956. In those days it was the general practice to load Home Trade grain cargoes according to the official 'Grain Letter'. This permitted a ship that did not completely fill up to load her bulk grain to the top of one end of the hold and to leave a sloping face at the other end. The sloping face was then secured by covering it with bags of grain, stepped into the bulk. This 'bagging' was not always carried out as diligently as it should have been and, in the absence of any real evidence, the inquiry considered that it had something to do with the ship's problem on this occasion. The accommodation was flooded when the ship took a heavy list causing sufficient concern for the Spurn Lifeboat to be launched and other ships to stand by including the *Shell Supplier* which pumped some oil to windward of the ship in an attempt to quell the force of the seas. Eventually, the *Stevonia* managed to reach the safety of the Royal Dock at Grimsby without further mishap.

The Trent Lighterage Company Ltd.

This company was incorporated on 7th July 1952 with a nominal capital of £5,000. Jack and Gladys Wharton were the first directors and were joined in 1954 by the company secretary, Stan Smith, the engineer superintendent Bill Muir and Mrs Joyce Gillies. The company was initially set up to control barge operations on the Trent and keep it separate from the coastal shipping of the parent company.

The work started with the purchase of the sloop *Christine* in 1948 which was later joined by the dumb barge *Ablen*. They carried coal from Hatfield Main Colliery staith between Thorne and Stainforth on the Stainforth and Keadby canal to the plant of Nitrogen Fertilisers Ltd. at Flixborough. The *Christine* carried about 100 tons of coal and the trip along the canal from Hatfield to Keadby would take just over four hours. Occasionally they would bring coal to the fertiliser works from Goole docks.

The *Christine* was built for John Simpson of Barton-on-Humber and originally named *Alva-S* after his daughter. The steel-built sloop had featured prominently in the traditional local sailing events and in 1926 had won the Barton Regatta. She was later sold to Fred Bingham and George Beevers of Rawcliffe, near Goole, who installed a 30 horse power Lister engine.

The keel *Freda* was purchased in 1950 from William Bleasdale and Co. Ltd. and shortly afterwards had a wheelhouse and a 30 horse power Lister engine installed by Browns Shipbuilding and Drydock Company at Hull. Both *Christine* and *Freda* were known as 'Sheffield Size' craft because their dimensions were 61'6" x 15'6" x 7'6" allowing them to negotiate the Tinsley Locks on the canal up to Sheffield. When the coal work to Flixborough ceased in the early 1960s the *Christine* was sold to Donald Downing of Beverley for further trading while the *Ablen* and *Freda* were probably scrapped.

Everard's *Firmity* at the Keadby coal staith. *[Company archives]*

The Dutch *Alja*, bought in 1958 and renamed *Trentonia*. *[J. and M. Clarkson]*

The company came into its own when the Scunthorpe slag merchants J.G. Eccles and Co. Ltd. consulted Whartons on the possibility of forming a shipping company and buying ships to carry their slag. An extraordinary general meeting was held at Railway Wharf on the 6th October 1958 when the authorised capital was increased to £15,000, later doubled to £30,000, with the slag merchants taking up half of the new equity. Shortly after the meeting, on 14th November 1958, the first ship was purchased for the company. She had been built in Groningen for the Buisman family in 1951 as the *Alja*. Renamed *Trentonia* she was soon integrated into the Wharton fleet and trading operations. In 1966 she was sold to Greek owners who took delivery at Greenhithe and after being sold to other Greek owners in 1974 she passed to a Colombian owner in 1978 and was registered in Panama. Her Bureau Veritas class was suspended in 1979, since when nothing official has been heard of the ship whose continued existence must be very doubtful.

The next acquisition by Trent Lighterage seems to have been an unlucky ship from the start. She was built at Alphen aan den Rijn as the *Jacoba M* for C. Brijder of Heemstede. He was having financial difficulties when the ship was completed in September 1958 and the builders retained the ship which was laid up until purchased at auction in January 1960. Maintaining the general style but with a local theme replacing the Wharton family names, the ship was renamed *Burtonia* after the village of Burton-upon-Stather where Jack Wharton made his home. Some re-commissioning work was carried out in Holland but the modifications required by the British government were carried out later at Greenhithe.

After a few years the shipment of slag declined and the interests in the company of J.G. Eccles waned accordingly. Following discussions in early 1975 Steven Wharton purchased all the shares held by Eccles and thereby gained full control of the company.

F.T. Everard and Sons Ltd.
A very important event took place on 15th July 1952 when an extraordinary general meeting of J. Wharton (Shipping) Ltd. was held in the Fenchurch Street offices of the well-known coastal shipowner F.T. Everard and Sons Ltd. The result was that the Everard family purchased half of the shares in J. Wharton (Shipping) Ltd. This gave a much needed injection of capital. The two companies had had many contacts over the years with Everard ships being regular callers at Keadby since the 1920s including the famous 'iron pot' sailing barges that loaded coal for the gas works at Margate.

Although members of the Everard family became directors of the company, Jack Wharton and later his son Steven were very much in control. The increased capital enabled the company to purchase Grove Farm at Gunness, about a mile downstream and on the opposite bank to Keadby. Planning permission was obtained for the building of jetties, storage areas and a small tank farm for the storage of petroleum products. Initially these tanks were served by Everard tankers, in particular the *Assiduity* (1,249/1964), for the account of Mobil Oil UK Ltd. The oil company needed such a facility in the Humber area until the Associated Petroleum Terminal came on stream at Immingham. Later, the bulk liquid storage terminal was leased to Tankfreight Ltd.

A wharf on the Grove Farm site was a new venture but there had been wharves at Gunness for well over a hundred years. Ironstone Wharf had been built to ship ironstone from the estate of Lord St. Oswald but much of this traffic later went to the railway. In a complete reversal of that early trade, several of the Trent wharves began to import ferro manganese concentrates and other raw materials for the local steel works during the 1970s. Just after the turn of the century the Yorkshire and Lincolnshire Tar Distillation Co. Ltd. established Gunness Wharf which carried on for many years although latterly it was mainly used as a dry cargo wharf. In addition to the early wharves there was also a landing stage where passengers and packets would be landed from the daily steamers of the Gainsborough United Steam Packet Co. Ltd.

The direct association with Everards was to have considerable influence on the company's affairs until it came to an amicable end in 1986. This influence and the effects will be noted in later sections of this narrative.

To be continued.

Burtonia. [Charles Hill]

Fleet list part 1

The list follows the usual Ships in Focus format, with the addition of port number and any relevant Commonwealth or foreign official numbers.

1. BRENDONIA (1) 1937-1939 1/1937
Goole.
O.N. 164894 313.13g 153.47n 400d
45.36 x 7.52 x 2.77 metres.
6-cyl. 4SCSA oil engine made by Humboldt-Deutz Motoren A.G., Koln, Germany, 280 x 450 mm; 200 kW, 9 knots.
12.4.1937: Completed by Goole Shipbuilding and Repairing Co. Ltd., Goole (Yard No. 325) for Jack Wharton, Keadby as BRENDONIA.
4.11.1938: Owner became J. Wharton (Shipping) Ltd., Keadby.
11.9.1939: Run down and sunk 1.5 miles west by south of the Gull Buoy by the British steamer ALDERPOOL (4,313/ 1936) while at anchor in the Downs awaiting a convoy. She was on passage from Goole to Fowey with a cargo of coal.

2. GLADONIA (1) 1939-1962 5/1939
Goole.
O.N. 164905 359.97g 178.02n 474d
45.56 x 7.52 x 2.99 metres.
6-cyl. 4SCSA oil engine made by Humboldt-Deutz Motoren A.G., Koln, Germany, 280 x 450 mm; 224 kW, 9 knots.
29.6.1939: Completed by Goole Shipbuilding and Repairing Co. Ltd., Goole (Yard No. 345) for J. Wharton (Shipping) Ltd., Keadby as GLADONIA.
9.1956: Re-engined with 6-cyl. 4SCSA oil engine made by Kloeckner-Humboldt-Deutz Motoren, A.G., Koln, West

Gladonia on the Thames with her masts lowered. *[J. and M. Clarkson]*

Germany, 320 x 450 mm; 300 kW, 9.5 knots.
23.1.1962: Stranded on sand banks south of the Hook of Holland while on passage from Par to Rotterdam with a cargo of china clay.
4.2.1962: Refloated and taken to a slipway at Capelle aan den Ijssel, Netherlands. Later declared a constructive total loss.
27.4.1962: Sold to Reederei J. Schoning, Haren-Ems, West Germany. Rebuilt by Jansen Schiffswerft & Maschinenfabrik, Leer, West Germany. Tonnages and dimensions became 420.28g, 219.39n, 566d, 49.78 x 7.52 x 2.99 metres.
11.5.1963: Re-entered service for Joseph Schoning, Haren-Ems, West Germany as MEIKE.
27.12.1967: Sold to Walter Pilar and Karl Gerdelman (Befrachtungskantoor Schoning G.m.b.H. managers), Leer, West Germany.
18.4.1968: Renamed WALKA.

18.3.1976: Sold to Thomas and Hall Trading Co. Ltd., Cayman Islands and renamed KIMBO. Registered 56/1976 in Georgetown; O.N. 373352.
15.5.1977: Sold to Centurion Shipping Ltd., Cayman Islands and renamed WALKA. Registered 55/1977 in Georgetown.
1978: Sold to Laja Lines S.A., Panama (Brown Trading Co., New Orleans, U.S.A., managers).
1980: Reported to have foundered off Panama.

3. BRENDONIA (2) 1945-1964 19/1941
Newcastle-upon-Tyne.
O.N. 165818 498.29g 250.48n 625d
51.59 x 8.11 x 3.25 metres.
6-cyl. 2SCSA oil engine made by Crossley Brothers Ltd., Manchester, 265 x 345 mm; 246 kW, 9 knots.
2.10.1941: Completed by Clelands (Successors) Ltd., Wallsend (Yard No. 57)

Brendonia (2). Note the alteration to the paintwork compared with the earlier aerial view. *[Charles Hill]*

Above: *Lizzonia* (1).   Below: *Stevonia* (1).   *[Both: J. and M. Clarkson collection]*

for the Ministry of War Transport (T.E. Evans and Co. Ltd., managers), London as EMPIRE HEAD. Registered 19/1941 in Newcastle-upon-Tyne.

1942: Manager became J. Wharton (Shipping) Ltd., Keadby.

20.9.1945: Acquired by J. Wharton (Shipping) Ltd., Keadby and renamed BRENDONIA. Registered 18/1945 in Goole.

5.1.1962: Re-engined with 6-cyl. 4SCSA oil engine made by Lister Blackstone Marine Ltd., Dursley, 222 x 292 mm; 373 kW, 8.5 knots.

13.7.1964: Sold to Nikolaos Dimitriadis & Compagnie, Piraeus, Greece and renamed IFIGENIA. Tonnages became 455g, 255n, 635d. Registered in Piraeus; O.N. 2434.

17.3.1972: Sold to Maninis Brothers (M. Fotopoulos, manager) Piraeus, Greece.

9.9.1976: Sold to Samin Mohamet, Arwad, Syria and renamed HAMZI. O.N. 1240.

19.1.1963: Found lying aground and abandoned at Golovasi, Yumurtalik Bay, Turkey having apparently drifted in ballast from a Syrian port. Subsequently refloated and taken over for disposal by the local port authority.

4. LIZZONIA (1) 1946-1961 21/1944 Goole.
O.N. 180125 409.77g 189.12n 450d
45.13 x 8.23 x 2.91 metres.
7-cyl. 4SCSA oil engine made by Blackstone and Co. Ltd., Stamford, 220 x 290 mm; 209 kW, 8 knots.

4.10.1944: Completed by Goole Shipbuilding and Repairing Co. Ltd.,

Goole (Yard No. 423) for the Ministry of War Transport, London (J.Wharton (Shipping) Ltd., Keadby, managers) as EMPIRE FAROUCHE.

1.4.1946: Owner became the Ministry of Transport, London.

22.7.1946: Acquired by J. Wharton (Shipping) Ltd., Keadby and renamed LIZZONIA.

1956: Re-engined with 6-cyl 4SCSA oil engine made by Blackstone and Co. Ltd., Stamford, 222 x 290 mm; 269 kW, 8.5 knots.

16.3.1961: Sank three miles west north west of the Varne Light Vessel after a collision in dense fog with the Swedish

motor vessel ARCTIC OCEAN (4,029/ 1948) whilst on passage from Antwerp to Plymouth with a cargo of potash.

5. STEVONIA (1) 1948-1961 1/1948 Goole.
O.N. 181203 383.97g 185.13n 447d 5.12 x 7.52 x 2.99 metres.
4-cyl 2SCSA oil engine made by British Polar Engines Ltd., Glasgow. 250 x 420 mm; 261 kW, 9 knots.

16.1.1948: Completed by Goole Shipbuilding and Repairing Co. Ltd., Goole (Yard No. 467) for J. Wharton (Shipping) Ltd., Keadby as STEVONIA.

The *River Avoca,* the former *Stevonia,* sailing from Eastham in July 1969. *[J. and M. Clarkson collection]*

Above: *Jackonia.* *[Tom Rayner]*

Jackonia, soon after being renamed *Iveragh,* arriving at Preston with a cargo of road stone from Penmaenmawr in North Wales. *[J. and M. Clarkson collection]*

6.12.1961: Sold to R.V.T. Hall, J. Tyrell and others, Arklow, Irish Republic and renamed RIVER AVOCA. Registered 12/1962 in Dublin; O.N. 400300.
12.1971: Re-engined with 6-cyl 4SCSA oil engine made by the Caterpillar Tractor Co., Peoria, U.S.A., 625 x 800 mm; 317 kW, 9 knots.
24.6.1976: Sold to Allyx Maritime Enterprises Inc., Panama and renamed RIVER KAROON.
12.1979: Sold to Frank Rijsdijk for demolition at Hendrik Ido Ambacht, Netherlands.
14.1.1980: Work commenced.

6. JACKONIA 1950-1963 1/1950 Goole.
O.N. 164614 412.69g 218.28n 525d
48.16 x 8.05 x 3.02 metres.
6-cyl 4SCSA oil engine made by Humboldt-Deutz Motoren A.G., Koln, Germany, 280 x 450 mm; 261 kW, 9 knots.
8.4.1936: Completed by Goole Shipbuilding and Repairing Co. Ltd., Goole (Yard No. 311) for S.G. Jenkings, London as CONIDA. Registered 62/1936 London.
26.1.1940: Sold to The Steamship Den of Airlie Co. Ltd. (Dundee, Perth and London Shipping Co. Ltd., managers), Dundee. Registered 4/1942 in Dundee.
5.11.1945: Transferred to Dundee, Perth and London Shipping Co. Ltd., Dundee and renamed DRON.
31.1.1950: Acquired by J. Wharton (Shipping) Ltd., Keadby and renamed JACKONIA. Registered 1/1950 in Goole.
3.5.1963: Sold to Transmarine International Ltd., Dublin, Irish Republic and renamed IVERAGH. Registered 20/1963 in Dublin, O.N. 400378.
1.10.1966: Sold to P.J. Tyrell, Arklow, Irish Republic.
3.1969: Sold to Hammond Lane Foundry Ltd. for demolition at Ringsend, Dublin, Irish Republic where she arrived on 20.3.1969.

7. TRYONIA 1954-1967 6/1954 Goole.
O.N. 181216 480.80g 243.77n 650d
47.30 x 8.56 x 3.42 metres.
8-cyl 4SCSA oil engine made by N.V. Appingedammer Brons, Appingedam, Netherlands, 290 x 450 mm; 373 kW, 10 knots.
11.1949: Completed by N.V. Bodewes Scheepswerven, Martenshoek, Netherlands (Yard No. 378) for Gebroeder C. & R. Tammes and Erven Tammes, Groningen, Netherlands as OCEAAN. Registered in Groningen.
17.7.1954: Acquired by J. Wharton (Shipping) Ltd., Keadby and renamed TRYONIA. Registered 6/1954 in Goole, O.N. 181216.
5.1.1967: Sold to George Mavros and others, Piraeus, Greece and renamed LITO. Registered in Piraeus, number 2939.

30.9.1967: Sold to Dotsiou Brothers (Mytikas Maritime Co. Ltd., managers), Piraeus, Greece.

1982: Re-engined with an 8-cyl. 4SCSA oil engine made by Kloeckner-Humboldt-Deutz A.G., Koln, West Germany, 320 x 450 mm; 368 kW, 9 knots.

22.11.1982: Re-registered in Salonika, O.N. 195.

5.12.1983: Sold to Alkyonis Shipping Co. Ltd., Valletta, Malta and renamed AGAPI. Provisionally registered in Malta, O.N. 0913.

5.4.1984: Last reported to have sailed from Piraeus.

4.11.1984: Maltese registration cancelled. Continued existence in doubt.

Two views of the *Tryonia*. *[Top: Tom Rayner, middle: J. and M. Clarkson collection]*

Managed for Ministry of War Transport

M1. EMPIRE HEAD 1942-1945.
See BRENDONIA (2).

M2. EMPIRE FAROUCHE 1944-1945.
See LIZZONIA (1).

Managed for Trent Lighterage Limited.

T1. TRENTONIA/TRENTONIA II
1958-1966 4/1958 Goole.
O.N. 300217 459.58g 358.90n 589d
49.51 x 8.18 x 3.11 metres.
6-cyl 4SCSA oil engine made by MaK. Maschinenbau Kiel A.G., Kiel, West Germany, 290 x 420 mm; 265 kW, 9 knots.
4.2.1951: Completed by N.V. Scheepsbouw Unie, Groningen, Netherlands (Yard No. 251) for Mrs Buisman-Van der Laan and A. and J. Buisman (J.J.Onnes, manager), Groningen, Netherlands as ALJA.

Trentonia (1). *[Dave Hocquard]*

162

14.11.1958: Acquired by Trent Lighterage Ltd. (J. Wharton (Shipping) Ltd., managers), Keadby and renamed TRENTONIA.
8.4.1964: Tonnages became 458.94g, 254.96n, 589d.
25.11.1964: Renamed TRENTONIA II.
18.11.1966: Sold to Stavros Skordalakis, G. Tsironis and Co., Piraeus, Greece and renamed CHALYPS.
12.6.1974: Sold to Emm. Ephstathiou (M. Fotopoulos, manager), Piraeus, Greece and renamed STELLA E.
19.10.1978: Sold to Unity Shipping Co. Ltd., Panama (M.A.Howard, Columbia, manager).
1997: Deleted from 'Lloyd's Register' as continued existence in doubt.

T2. BURTONIA 1960-1972 1/1960 Goole.
O.N. 300222 498.03g 341.13n 680d
54.36 x 8.71 x 3.15 metres.
6-cyl 4SCSA oil engine made by D. & J. Boot Motorenfabriek 'De Industrie', Alphen aan den Rijn, Netherlands, 305 x 460 mm; 336 kW, 9 knots.
27.9.1958: Completed by D. & J. Boot Scheepswerf 'De Vooruitgang', Alphen aan den Rijn, Netherlands (Yard No. 1260) for C. Brijder, Heemstede, Netherlands as JACOMA M. but owner could not take delivery due to financial difficulties.
28.1.1960: Acquired at public auction by Trent Lighterage Ltd. (J. Wharton (Shipping) Ltd., managers), Keadby and renamed BURTONIA.
14.4.1964: Tonnages became 498.03g, 288.51n, 680d.
30.11.1972: Listed, capsized and sank off Southwold in position 53.23 north by

Trentonia II in the Bristol Channel. [W. D. Harris/J. and M. Clarkson collection]

01.55 east in a severe storm while on passage from Keadby to Ghent with a cargo of lead concentrates.

Inland waterways craft

IW1. CHRISTINE 1952-1967 Steel sloop 45/1953 Hull.
O.N. 148407 67.98g 67.98n 61.5 x 15.5 x 7.6 feet
24.11.1924: Completed by W.H. Warren, New Holland for John G. Simpson, Barton-on-Humber as ALVA S. Registered 78/1924 in Hull.
18.10.1943: Sold to Frederick Bingham (32/64), Goole and George Beevers (32/64), Rawcliffe.
24.6.1952: Acquired by Trent Lighterage Ltd., Keadby.
8.8.1952: Fitted with a 3-cyl. 4SCSA oil engine made by Lister Marine Ltd., Dursley. Tonnages became 67.95g, 61.30n.

1953: Renamed CHRISTINE and registered *de novo* 45/1953 in Hull.
1967: Sold to Donald Downing, Beverley.
1973: Demolished in the Humber area.

IW2. ABLEN 1965-19— Dumb barge 11/1942 Hull.
O.N. 167117 53.84g 50.84n 57.2 x 14.5 x 7.3 feet.
1899: Completed by Henry Scarr, Beverley for Flixborough Shipping Ltd., Flixborough as ABLEN.
1.10.1953: Sold to C. Beckett, Thorne.
2.10.1965: Acquired by Trent Lighterage Ltd., Keadby.
No further details.

IW3. FREDA Steel keel
100d 61.5 x 15.5 x 7.6 feet.
Unregistered and formerly owned by William Bleasdale and Co. Ltd., Hull. Lister engine fitted after purchase.

Burtonia. [Dave Hocquard]

UNDER THE STAR AND CRESCENT:
BRITISH-BUILT SHIPS OWNED IN PAKISTAN - Part 2
Peter Myers

IQBALBAKSH (below)

Barclay, Curle and Co. Ltd., Whiteinch, Glasgow; 1940, 6,854g, 442 feet
T. 3-cyl. by Barclay, Curle and Co. Ltd., Whiteinch, Glasgow.

The *Iqbalbaksh* was originally the *Itria* (below), the only one of British India's seven-member 'I' class not to have been built at William Gray's West Hartlepool yard. She entered service with the Ministry of War Transport's Liner Division on completion and spent most of her uneventful wartime career transporting military equipment. She entered service with British India in March 1946 and served the company until she was sold to the United Oriental Steamship Co. on 11th July 1958. The *Iqbalbaksh* was one of nine ships owned by the company in the mid-1960s. She was laid up in 1970 and in 1971 was sold for demolition in Pakistan.

FATEHABAD

William Gray and Co. Ltd., West Hartlepool; 1940, 6,793gt, 442 feet
T. 3-cyl. with low pressure turbine and double reduction gearing by Central Marine Engineering Works, Hartlepool.

The *Fatehabad* was another of British India's 'I' class which was acquired by Pakistani owners, her original name being the *Ikauna*. She was delivered in March 1941 and in January 1945 served as an army vehicle transport at the Kyaukpyu landings in Burma. She was sold to Pakistan in July 1958 and in the following year she had been renamed *Fatehabad* by her owners, the Pakistan Steam Navigation Co. Ltd. of Chittagong. This firm had also acquired British India's *Itaura* (6,793gt/1940) which became their *Jahangiribad*. Both ships passed to the East Bengal Steam Ship Co., Chittagong, in 1965. The *Jahangiribad* was broken up in 1969, while the *Fatehabad* was scrapped in May 1968. The two other 'I' class ships purchased by Pakistani shipowners were the *Pakistan Promoter*, ex-*Itola* 1958 (6,793gt/1940) of the Karachi Steam Navigation Co. and the *Safina-e-Jamhooriyat*, ex-*Ismailia* 1958, of the Pan-Islamic Steamship Co. Ltd.

Ikauna [J. and M. Clarkson]

Fatehabad.   [J. and M. Clarkson]

Itaura. [J. and M. Clarkson]

Itola. [J. and M. Clarkson]

Ismailia became the *Safina-e-Jamhooriyat.* *[J. and M. Clarkson]*

ILYASBAKSH (below)
Caledon Shipbuilding and Engineering Co.
Ltd., Dundee; 1943, 7,038gt, 431 feet
T. 3-cyl. by North Eastern Marine
Engineering Co. (1938) Ltd., Newcastle-
upon-Tyne
The *Ilyasbaksh* was another of United
Oriental's fleet that was of wartime origin
and had been completed for the Ministry of
War Transport as the *Empire Canyon*, a B
type partially pre-fabricated standard cargo
steamship. She was managed by F.C. Strick
and Co. Ltd. between 1943 and 1946 when
Capper, Alexander and Co. Ltd. took over
her management. This company acquired
her in 1947 and she was renamed
Holmbury. She became the *Ilyasbaksh* in
1960 after she was bought by United
Oriental but in 1966 she was seized by the
Indian Government in the aftermath of the
Indo-Pakistan War of 1965 and was
scrapped at Bombay in 1970.

Above: *Holmbury.* *[W.H. Brown/J.& M. Clarkson collection]*
Below: *Ilyasbaksh.* *[Peter Newall collection]*

Haringhata seen here in the Mersey as Clan Lines' Clan MacKendrick. [B. & A. Feilden/J. & M. Clarkson collection]

HARINGHATA

John Readhead and Sons Ltd., South Shields; 1943, 7,068gt, 431 feet
T. 3-cyl, built by John Readhead and Sons Ltd., South Shields.

This ship was another example of the B type partially fabricated standard cargo steamship built for the Ministry of War Transport and was originally *Empire Pickwick,* and sailed in Convoy JW 55A from Loch Ewe to Murmansk in December 1943. She was managed by Donaldson Brothers and Black until 1946 when Cayzer, Irvine and Co. Ltd. took over her management. She was bought by The Clan Line Steamers Ltd. in 1948 and renamed *Clan Mackendrick.* In 1961 she was sold to Mullion and Co., Hong Kong, and became their *Ardpatrick.* The National Shipping Corporation, of Karachi, bought her in 1966 and renamed her *Haringhata,* but she did not last long in their service and arrived at her home port for scrapping in July 1968. Two other former *Empire* ships which also had brief careers in the 1960s with the National Shipping Corporation were the *Kaukhali,* ex-*Inchmay* 1966, ex-*Corrientes* 1955, ex-*Empire Cromer* 1946 (7,075gt/1944), and the *Tetulia,* ex-*Inchleana* 1966, ex-*Oregon Star* 1955, ex-*Gracia* 1954, ex-*Empire Treasure* 1946 (7,040gt/1943).

ISLAMABAD

Cochrane and Sons Ltd., Selby, 1945; 395gt, 144 feet
T. 3-cyl by Amos and Smith Ltd., Hull.
The *Islamabad* started her career as the *Empire Mayring,* one of 14 C-type dry cargo coasters built for the Ministry of War Transport and designed specially for service in the Far East. She remained out east when she was bought in 1947 by the Ta Hing Co. (Mollers Ltd., Hong Kong)

Above: *Haringhata. [D. H. Johnzon collection/Ships in Focus]*
Below: Donaldson's *Corrientes* of 1944 became the *Kaukhali. [J. & M. Clarkson collection]*

and renamed *Sing Hing.* She passed to Wallem and Co., Hong Kong, in 1949 before she was bought by the Pakistan Steam Navigation Co. Ltd., Chittagong in 1951 and renamed *Islamabad.* She was sold to the Bangladesh Steam Navigation Co. Ltd. (A.K. Khan and Co., managers), also of Chittagong, in 1972. Although she is still listed in 'Lloyd's Register', it is more than likely that she no longer exists. Unfortunately no photographs have been found of this vessel.

SAFINA- E-AHMAR

Blyth Shipbuilding and Dry Dock Co. Ltd., Blyth; 1945, 906gt, 215 feet
T. 3-cyl, built by George Clark (1938) Ltd., Sunderland.

The *Safina-e-Ahmar* began life as the *Empire Pavilion*, one of the seven B-type shelter deck type coasters built for the Ministry of War Transport and designed specially for service in the Far East and which were capable of carrying a small number of troops in the 'tween decks. She was managed for the Ministry of War Transport by Elder Dempster before becoming that company's *Sapele* in 1946 and for whom she traded along the West African coast. She was sold in 1963 to Bergens Mek. Verkstad, but was quickly resold to Ocean Industries Ltd. of Karachi, who renamed her *Mahia* and had her converted to a shrimp factory ship, with a new gross tonnage of 1,359. She passed to the Pan-Islamic Steamship Co. Ltd. in 1969, becoming their *Safina-e-Ahmar*, and was converted back to a dry cargo ship with a gross tonnage of 906. She arrived for breaking up at Karachi on 22nd March 1973.

MAQBOOLBAKSH

Bartram and Sons Ltd., Sunderland; 1945, 7,449gt, 449 feet
T. 3-cyl. by North Eastern Marine Engineering Co. (1938) Ltd., Sunderland.

The *Maqboolbaksh* was originally British India's *Pemba*, which was completed at the end of 1945 and converted to oil-firing in 1946. She was one of a number of former British India cargo ships which remained in eastern waters after their sale to Pakistani owners. United Oriental bought her on 6th January 1960 and based her at Chittagong. She served the firm for a creditable 12 years until sold for breaking up in Pakistan in 1972.

Above: *Safina-e-Ahmar* as the *Sapele*. [Ships in Focus]

Above: British India Line's *Pemba* in the River Thames in May 1955 and below under the Pakistan flag as *Maqboolbaksh*. [Ian Farquhar collection]

SAFINA-E-BARKAT
Short Brothers Ltd., Sunderland; 1947,
5,391gt, 420.5 feet
T. 3-cyl. by George Clark (1938) Ltd.,
Sunderland.

The *Safina-e-Barkat* was built originally as
the *Blankvann* for Norwegian owners
Blankvann D/S A/S Vard (Jacobsen and
Salvesen) of Oslo, and indicative of a time
when British shipyards were busy
replacing lost wartime tonnage not only
for UK companies but for foreign ones as
well. The Pan-Islamic company bought
her in 1959 and she served them until sold
for demolition at Karachi in March 1972.

MUSTALI (2)
Short Brothers Ltd., Sunderland; 1948,
5,670gt, 441 feet
T. 3-cyl. by George Clark (1938) Ltd.,
Sunderland.

This ship was built as the *Rigoletto* for
Rederi A/B Soya (O. Wallenius, manager)
of Sweden before passing to another
Swedish owner, Rederiet for S.S. Artemis
(Lars Gabrielson, manager) in 1954 and
was renamed *Artemis*. She became the
Mustali after she was acquired in 1960 by
Gulf Steamships Ltd., Karachi. The firm
became a public limited company in May
1970 and their title was changed to Gulf
Shipping Corporation Ltd. The *Mustali*
became a casualty of the Bangladesh War
when she was set on fire and sunk by
Indian Air Force bombers on 9th
December 1971 while lying at Chalna,
East Pakistan. From a crew of 52, her
master and 10 crew members were killed.
Her wreck was later removed and broken
up.

Blankvann at Port Said in 1955. *[J. & M. Clarkson collection]*

Above: *Safina-e-Barkat* in 1962 in a United States port. *[Ships in Focus]*
Below: *Mustali*. *[Roy Fenton collection]*

169

SAFINA-E-NUSRAT

John Readhead and Sons Ltd., South Shields; 1949, 5,815gt, 435 feet
T. 3-cyl by John Readhead and Sons Ltd., South Shields with low pressure turbine double reduction gearing and hydraulic coupling

The *Tregenna* was one of three steamships built for the Hain Steamship Co. Ltd. in 1949, but the *Tregenna, Treglisson and Tregothnan* were to prove uneconomic and were sold to Karachi shipowners within ten years of delivery. The *Tregenna* was sold for £205,000 to the Pan-Islamic Steamship Co. Ltd. in December 1959 and renamed *Safina-e-Nusrat.* She served her new owners for 16 years before being sold to Pakistani shipbreakers after her arrival at Karachi in November 1975. Her demolition started in June 1976 at Gadani Beach, where the Pan-Islamic's well-known pilgrim ship S*afina-e-Hujjaj* (19,116/35) ex-*Empire Fowey* 1960, ex *Potsdam* 1946 was also broken up that year.

YOUSUF BAKSH

Wm. Hamilton and Co. Ltd., Port Glasgow; 1949, 5,270gt, 435 feet
T. 3-cyl. by D. Rowan and Co. Ltd., Glasgow, with low pressure turbine double reduction gearing and hydraulic coupling.

Hain's *Treglisson* became the *Yousuf Baksh* of the United Oriental Steamship Co. in March 1960. The carriage of jute from East Pakistan was a staple export cargo for Pakistani ships, but jute, unfortunately, could be a fire hazard. The *Yousuf Baksh* made the headlines on 8th May 1965 after fire broke out in her cargo of jute while on a voyage from Chittagong to Boulogne, London, Dundee and Antwerp. She anchored off Deal, Kent, and was later beached on Sandwich Flats after her crew had been taken off by the Walmer lifeboat and in the ship's own boats. The German salvage tugs *Hermes* and *Heros* helped in fighting the fire with the Kent Fire Brigade. The fire was subdued after nearly 48 hours, but by that time the ship below decks was a smouldering mass of jute, oilcake and cotton. There was also extensive damage to the *Yousuf Baksh*'s superstructure and to her hull plating. On 1st June she arrived in tow at Rotterdam where her cargo was discharged. She was found to be beyond economical repair and sold to German shipbreakers at Hamburg where demolition started in January 1966.

Top and upper middle*: Tregenna* in 1957 and a well painted *Safina-e-Nusrat* in May 1966.
Lower middle and bottom: *Yousuf Baksh* with the tugs *Hermes* and *Heros* alongside. In the lower picture, dated 12th May 1965, smoke or steam can be seen coming from the forward hold. *[All J. & M. Clarkson collection]*

OCEAN ENTERPRISE

John Readhead and Sons Ltd., South Shields; 1949, 5,851gt, 435 feet
T. 3-cyl. by John Readhead and Sons Ltd., South Shields with low pressure turbine, double reduction gearing and hydraulic coupling.

Hain's *Tregothnan* was sold for £207,500 to the Dinshaw family's Trans Oceanic Steam Ship Co., Karachi, in 1959 and renamed *Ocean Enterprise*. In August 1965 she loaded jute for Dundee at Chittagong and Chalna before sailing for Calcutta to load manufactured jute goods. It was while there that she was impounded by the Indian Government on 6th September after war broke out between India and Pakistan. Her Pakistani crew were interned, but not her master and chief

engineer, who were British citizens. The raw jute from East Pakistan remained aboard the *Ocean Enterprise* until it was discharged in July 1966. Some of the consignees decided to cut their losses by selling their jute to mills in Calcutta. On 9th December 1971 the *Ocean Enterprise* was heavily damaged during Indian air attacks while lying at Chalna during the Indo-Pakistan War. There were no reports about her fate, but it was assumed that she was later broken up.

DACCA CITY

William Gray and Co. Ltd., West Hartlepool; 1949, 5,368gt; 421 feet
T. 3-cyl. by Central Marine Engineering Works, Hartlepool.

The *Dacca City* was built as the *Irish Plane* for the Irish Shipping Co. Ltd., Dublin, and was bought by the Chittagong Steamship Corporation, Chittagong in 1960, joining that company's *Chittagong City*. She was sold for breaking up at Karachi in March 1971.

Top: *Tregothnan* in a South Wales port. Note the army vehicles including ambulances stowed on deck. *[J. & M. Clarkson collection]*
Middle: After being sold and renamed *Ocean Enterprise*. *[Roy Fenton collection]*
Below: The *Irish Plane* was sold by Irish Shipping in 1960 and renamed *Dacca City*. *[J. & M. Clarkson collection]*

KAREEM

Henry Robb and Co. Ltd., Leith; 1949,
2,213gt, 266 feet
5-cyl. oil engine by British Polar Engines
Ltd., Glasgow.

The *Kareem* was built as the twin-screw
passenger and cargo liner *Mombasa* for the
British India Steam Navigation Co. Ltd. for
their East African coastal service. When
completed she had accommodation for
eight first-saloon and 16 second-saloon
passengers as well as 150 deck passengers.
The *Mombasa* had carried 200,000
passengers and 250,000 tons of cargo when
she left Dar es Salaam on her final voyage
on 16th August 1960. In October 1961 she
was bought by Crescent Shipping Lines
Ltd., Karachi and renamed *Kareem.*
Pakistani cotton merchants had established
this company in 1960 and which had taken
delivery that year of the Osaka-built
passenger/general cargo ship *Shams* for the
trade between West and East Pakistan. It is
believed that the *Kareem* was used for a
coastal service until she was sold for
demolition in 1968.

SURMA

William Gray and Co. Ltd., West
Hartlepool; 1951, 5,890gt, 456 feet
T. 3-cyl. Central Marine Engine Works,
West Hartlepool.

This ship was built as the *Seawall* for
Matapan Shipping Co. Ltd. (Lykiardopulo
and Co. Ltd., managers) of London. She
was purchased in 1955 by the British Steam
Shipping Co. Ltd. of Cardiff (John Cory
and Sons Ltd., managers) and renamed
Ramillies, being the only ship owned by the
company at that time. She was sold to the
National Shipping Corporation of Karachi
in 1966 and renamed *Surma,* but just five
years later she became a victim of Indian air
strikes on or about 16th December, 1971,
while lying at Chalna, and after the Indo-
Pakistan War she was found sunk and
beyond salvage.

ANISBAKSH

Smith's Dock Co. Ltd., Middlesbrough;
1952, 6,273gt, 451 feet
T. 3-cyl. by Smith's Dock Co. Ltd.,
Middlesbrough.

Another British-built cargo steamer bought
by the United Oriental Steamship Co. was
the *Ramsay* in 1960, previously owned by
the Bolton Steam Shipping Co. Ltd. of
London. She was renamed *Anisbaksh* but
was fated to be a casualty of the Indo-
Pakistan War of December 1971. She was
bombed and sunk at Chittagong by Sea
Hawk jets from the Indian Navy aircraft
carrier *Vikrant.* She was later raised and
scrapped at a yard about 20 miles from
Chittagong in 1972.

AL MURTAZA (right)

Furness Shipbuilding Co. Ltd., Haverton
Hill-on-Tees; 1955, 8,299gt, 436 feet

Mombasa fitting out at Leith. *[David Whiteside collection]*

Kareem. [Peter Newall collection]

Surma. [Peter Newall collection]

4-cyl. oil engine by Hawthorn Leslie and
Co. Ltd., Newcastle-upon-Tyne.
The *Al Murtaza* was one of the few
British-built ships owned by the
Muhammadi Steamship Co. Ltd. of
Karachi, which was incorporated on 13th
May 1947. Mohammad Ali Jinnah, the
founding father of Pakistan, sought the
assistance of Rustom Cowasjee, the senior
partner of the East and West Steamship
Co., in helping Mahomed Ali Seth in
setting up the Muhammadi company. The
company's first ships were time chartered,
but once established their first purchases
were wartime, Canadian-built standard
ships. The *Al Murtaza* was built as the
President Kruger for Northern Steamships
Ltd., Johannesburg and was sold in 1959
to briefly become the *Neptun,* of Union
Kabel-legungs und Schiffahrts G.m.b.H.,
Nordenhem, West Germany, before being
acquired by Muhammadi in 1960. She
passed to the Pakistan Shipping
Corporation in 1974 and traded for them
until sold for breaking up at Karachi in
November 1979.

Ramsay in 1953. *[J. & M. Clarkson collection]*

Anisbaksh in the Singapore Straits on the 15th July 1970. *[J. & M. Clarkson collection]*

Al Murtaza. [Roy Fenton collection]

General arrangement plan.

174

BARTELS
Colin Turner

Towards the end of the First World War there was an increased interest in the use of steel reinforced concrete as a material for building ships. The obvious advantages lay in the potential for the saving of steel and in the quickness of build. In Great Britain some tugs and barges were constructed of the material, but the only large ship to be built was the steamer *Armistice* (894/1919). In the United States of America the medium was pursued more vigorously and several designs were prepared for both dry cargo ships, of various deadweights, and for a class of tankers of 7,500 tons deadweight. Inevitably the end of hostilities removed the impetus from the programme and in the event only eight tankers were completed, together with a few dry cargo ships of 3,500 tons deadweight. Of the tankers, only four entered revenue-earning service and these were soon withdrawn for various reasons, not least of which was the fact that their low deadweight capacity, for the size of the ship, made them commercially unattractive in peacetime trading conditions.

In Europe, the engineer N.K. Fougner had pioneered ferro-concrete shipbuilding when he produced the 84-foot motor ship *Namsenfjord* in 1917, which was followed by two others, each slightly larger. However, perhaps the most interesting of the concrete ships dating from this era was the Danish designed and built *Bartels*, which at the time held title as the largest concrete ship built in Europe. She was built by Nordisk Handels-og Ingeniørvirksomhed A/S Cyclone (Højgaard & Schultz, managers) in co-operation with the Copenhagen Drydock Company. The hull structure was designed by Knud Bartels, who had worked with Højgaard in Russia in 1917, and was of a form that he patented later as the 'System Bartels'. The ship was completed on the 2nd June 1920, having taken almost two years to construct.

Fate was particularly unkind to Bartels, for in October 1918, when the contract was signed for the construction of the ship, he was amongst the millions who lost their lives in the Spanish Influenza pandemic. He was only 33 years old.

The *Bartels* was 239 feet 9 inches between perpendiculars, with a beam of 36 feet 6 inches and a depth of 20 feet 6 inches. Her gross tonnage was 1,249 with a deadweight in the region of 1,800 tons including bunkers of 219 tons. A triple expansion steam engine, with cylinder diameters of 15", 24" and 40" and a 27" stroke, gave her a top speed of 8 knots. At this speed she consumed 7.5 tons of coal per day. She carried three derricks, two on her foremast and one on a stump mainmast; these served three hatches each of which measured 26 feet by 15 feet. Her profile was very modern for the time, in that her superstructure and engines were placed aft. Unusually, she was built with a cross section that resembled the trunk and turret forms that had long since fallen out of favour. The *Bartels* was, however, neither a turret nor a trunk deck steamer in the strictest sense, but had more in common with the Priestman Tower Deck design, in so far as the narrow upper deck sloped down at an angle of about 45 degrees to meet a lower harbour deck. The thickness of the

concrete that formed the shell of the hull was in the region of 3¹/₂ inches, and this produced one of the lightest concrete hulls built at that time.

Knud Bartels had incorporated a double bottom in his design, in which the floor of the hold was supported above the ship's bottom by a series of inverted, V-shaped beams. This double bottom was divided into four main ballast tanks. Fougner in his book 'Seagoing and other Concrete Ships' remarks that this double bottom was of questionable value as it reduced deadweight and necessitated extra pumping and pipelines when there was no need for ballast tanks in concrete ships, other than for fore and aft trimming. His preference would have been for a massive bottom slab, say 6 or 7 inches in thickness rather than the 3.5 inches that had been used. Fougner also expressed the view that the complicated nature of the double bottom and the 'turret' deck, particularly in the fabrication of the steel bars which formed the skeletal frame of the ship, had amounted to labour which was much above the norm for concrete ships. In that the *Bartels* took almost two years to complete, he may well have been correct.

The *Bartels* was named and launched on the 30th January 1920, and undertook her trials on the 2nd June. The following day she was delivered to A/S Dampskibsselskabet Patria (Torben Neilsen, manager) of Copenhagen and was placed in the coal trade with British north-eastern ports. Five

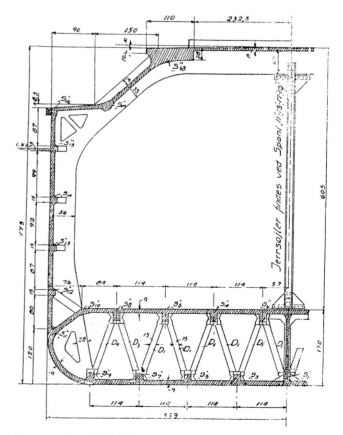

Cross section of *Bartels*.

months later, at 7.20 a.m. on the 12th November, the fully loaded *Bartels* ran aground on the island of Hjelm, at a point known locally as Stonefishermens' Paradise, when nearing the end of a passage from Methil to Aarhus.

Having struck at full speed, the ship was firmly grounded from the bow to the bridge superstructure. The crew's efforts to free the ship were unavailing and, with the forepeak and tanks 1 and 2 flooded, assistance was requested. This arrived at 11.30 p.m. in the form of the salvage steamer *Kattegat*. However, weather conditions did not allow any attempts at re-floating the *Bartels* until 18th November, when the coal cargo began to be off loaded into barges. From her grounding to the commencement of salvage operations the *Bartels* had been subjected to a heavy pounding by a swell whipped up by force 6 to 7 winds, resulting in further bottom damage that allowed the flooding to extend to tanks 3 and 4. At 7.15 a.m. on the 23rd November the *Bartels* was refloated and towed into Aarhus to be dry-docked for inspection. The survey revealed that in the areas of greatest damage the concrete was completely missing, leaving the steel reinforcement totally exposed, whilst in other areas the concrete hull was cracked and scored. A number of indentations of a depth of 2 centimetres and a diameter of 30 centimetres were also discovered in the bottom in the region

Bartels in one of the two building docks at the shipyard - Sondre Vaerft, the Southern Shipyard, during her naming ceremony on 30th January 1920. *[Soren Thorsoe collection]*

of number 3 tank, which had resulted from her pounding against the stones which littered the seabed at the point of her grounding. The exposed steelwork was largely undamaged, except for some areas where it had been forced inwards by up to 15 centimetres. The double bottom had, however, proved its worth, as the tank tops were undamaged and no flooding of the holds and engine room had occurred.

Bartels in the Nordre Vaerft, the Northern Shipyard prior to completion. *[Soren Thorsoe collection]*

Bartels heading through the port of Copenhagen for sea trials in the Sound on 2nd June 1920 - completion day. *[Soren Thorsoe collection]*

In his description of the *Bartels*, Fougner refers to the grounding and concedes that the double bottom did indeed keep water out of the holds but wondered whether any leaks would have occurred if a simple massive bottom slab had been used instead. The repairs were carried out by the original builders, who commenced cutting away the damaged concrete on 17th December; the repairs being completed 21 working days later on 12th January. In the course of the repairs approximately one third of the bottom was replaced (165 square metres). The most difficult aspect of the work concerned the repair of the steel

reinforcement. Those areas where the steel had been deformed had to be cut out and new steel inserted. To achieve this it was often necessary to cut out undamaged sections of concrete. The *Bartels* was undocked eight days after the final concreting and returned to service. The repairers felt that the saving of working hours over similar repairs to a steel ship was of the order 4.5 to 1. Herein lay perhaps the only advantage of ferro-concrete over that of conventional steel construction.

Like every other seagoing concrete ship, the *Bartels* did not enjoy a long commercial life. Between April and

The *Bartels* in service. *[Danish Maritime Museum, Elsinore]*

Bartels at sea. The turret-like nature of her hull is apparent. *[Danish Maritime Museum, Elsinore]*

November 1921 she was laid up at Copenhagen, her ownership being transferred to O. Ovesen in 1922. In 1924 the *Bartels* was in the hands of the shipbuilders Howaldtswerke of Kiel, to whom she had been sold in what was probably a part exchange deal, given that her engines and boilers were installed in the steamship *Bryssel* (1924/1,271) which was then under construction at the yard for Ovesen. The *Bryssel* underwent many changes of name and ownership being scrapped as the Greek owned *Philippos* in 1965. The hull of *Bartels* was sold to Ekensberg Varf A/B of Stockholm to become a storage barge. In 1983, after having further registration refused by the Swedish Register, the *Bartels* embarked on a new career as an accommodation ship. A two-decked superstructure was added that almost completely filled the length of the upper deck between the forecastle and the poop; the rooms thus created were hired out to local businesses. Somewhat bizarrely this deckhouse was topped-off amidships with a false funnel. In 1984 she was renamed *Hantverkaren*. The *Hantverkaren* continued in her role until 1994, when she was sold to a Norwegian company, only to founder on the 30th June off the northern point of Öland whilst under tow. In her latter career the *Bartels* was not untypical of other concrete ships, whose hulls showed immense strength and longevity. Many were utilised to provide floating breakwaters or storage facilities. Indeed, two of her contemporaries, the US tankers *Peralta* and *San Pasqual* are still afloat, the former as a breakwater in the Powell River, British Columbia, and the latter as a hotel in Cuba.

The *Bartels* after conversion into an accomodation ship and moored in Stockholm, Sweden in May 1986. *[Olle Renck/Soren Thorsoe collection]*

SAILING TANKERS
Part 3: later conversions
John Naylon

Belief in the economic viability of sailing bulk tankers continued well into the twentieth century, bolstered by the exponential growth in demand for oil created by the invention of the internal combustion engine. Indeed, the largest sailing vessel ever built, Prentout-Leblond's five-masted barque *France* (2) of 1911, was conceived as a bulk tanker for the transatlantic trade, although in fact she spent her life in the New Caledonian nickel ore trade. This confidence occasioned the conversion of five notable sailing ships. Three of them were the biggest of their kind and four were built by Russell and Co. of Port Glasgow. These were sail's last contribution to bulk oil transport.

Thomas W. Lawson

The world's only seven-masted schooner and the largest non-auxiliary sailing ship, the *Lawson* was the brainchild of Captain John G. Crowley, manager of the Coastwise Transportation Company of Boston. She was built to meet the need for ever-larger hulls to carry coal along the eastern United States seaboard, a trade being lost to the railways through the increasing running costs of American ships, and to overcome the inherent weakness of excessively long wooden hulls. Other multi-masted steel schooners included the six-masted *William L. Douglas*, also brought out by Captain Crowley and built like the *Lawson* at Quincy, Massachusetts, in 1902, and the five-masted *Kineo*, built by Sewall and Co. at Bath, Maine, in 1903. Indeed, the construction of an eight-masted schooner was discussed in the *Nautical Gazette*.

Unique and impressive but no beauty, the *Lawson* was designed – somewhat ironically – by Bowdoin B. Crowninshield, best known as a yacht designer (the 1901 America's Cup contender *Independence*) but also the architect of commercial fishing and coasting schooners, and was named for the New England financier who was a principal backer in the vessel. She was launched on 10th July 1902 by the Fore River Ship and Engine Building Co. of Quincy at a cost of

The *Thomas W. Lawson*'s seven masts were not, as sometimes suggested, called after the days of the week. They were fore, main, mizzen, spanker, jigger, driver and pusher (albeit not always in that order). *[Stebbins, Boston/San Francisco Maritime National Historical Park, J. Porter Shaw collection J7.26,279n]*

$240,000. Her dimensions of 395.0 feet overall, 50.0 feet beam, 32.9 feet depth, 5,218gt, 4,912nt and deadweight of over 8,000 tons made her the third largest sailing vessel of any kind. She was built of steel throughout, except for her Oregon pine topmasts. The seven lower masts, of 38 inches diameter, were 135 feet long and carried 58-foot topmasts, giving a mast weight of 20 tons. Together with an 85-foot bowsprit they bore 40,617 square feet of canvas. Ballast tanks in the four-foot-deep double bottom and fore and aft peak tanks enabled her to load 1,069 tons of water ballast on a draught of 12 feet. With economy in mind, halyards and topping lifts were led to two steam winches, one forward and one on the aft deckhouse, so that this giant could be worked by only 16-18 men, who also benefited from steam-assisted steering gear, steam-heated quarters, electricity and a telephone system.

The *Lawson* was built to carry coal from Hampton Roads to New England ports, usually Boston or Portland. She could load 7,500 tons on a draught of 26 feet and 9,200 tons on 29 feet 10 inches. She was not, however, a success in her intended role. With such a draught her choice of port was limited; Newport News was the only place where she could lie afloat fully loaded and she went aground several times. Despite her steam-assisted steering and sail handling she was difficult to manage with her small crew. In ballast she was impossible to tack and had to be jibed over or even – reputedly – club-hauled.

Not surprisingly, then, low freights caused her to be withdrawn from the coal trade in 1904 and sold to Standard Oil of New Jersey, who sent her to Newport News for conversion to a bulk tanker. Fourteen tanks were installed to carry 2.5 million gallons of oil, and for the rest of her short coastwise career she was stripped of her topmasts and towed as a barge between Port Arthur, Texas, and Marcus Hook, Philadelphia, under charter to the Sun Oil Company.

Her end came tragically in 1907 on her first attempted transatlantic passage. With her topmasts refitted and a crew of 18, she left Marcus Hook for London on 27th November with 2,003,063 gallons of lubricating oil on behalf of Anglo-American. Tempestuous weather was encountered from the start. During a 17-day crossing her decks were continuously swept, hatches stove in, boats smashed and lost, sails blown out, and oil had to be pumped overboard from the aftermost tank since she was settling by the stern. On Friday 13th December, mistaking his landfall, Captain George W. Dow found himself close inshore off the Scillies, among rocks and reefs near the Bishop Rock Lighthouse. With no room to manoeuvre and in a violent north westerly gale, the *Lawton* was brought-to and put both anchors out. As a precautionary measure the St. Agnes and St. Mary's lifeboats offered to take off the crew but Captain Dow declined, requesting a tug instead. During the early hours of 14th December both cables parted; the ship went onto Heleweather reef off Annet island, broke in two between the sixth and seventh masts, rolled over and sank. There were only three survivors: Captain Dow, engineer Edward L. Rowe and seaman George Allen, who later died of his injuries. Fifteen men were drowned, plus pilot William Cook Hicks, who had been put aboard the previous night by the St. Agnes lifeboat.

Captain William Matson (1849-1917)

The next two conversions – *Falls of Clyde* and *Marion Chilcott* – were associated with Captain William Matson, a pioneer in the Hawaiian sugar trade and a heavy investor in the southern Californian oil industry. It was Captain Matson who in the early twentieth century introduced oil as a fuel for machinery on the Hawaiian plantations, replacing the coal formerly brought from Newcastle, New South Wales, at twice the cost. From 1882 onwards he acquired 21 sailing vessels, mostly elderly ships at advantageous prices. These included not only American square riggers and schooners but also British-built iron and steel vessels: the barques *Ada Iredale* (1872), *Santiago* (1885), *Andrew Welch* (1888) and *R.P. Rithet* (1892); the four-masted barques *Fort George* (1884) and *Hawaiian Isles* (1892); and the full riggers *Roderick Dhu* (1874), *Cypromene* (1878), *Falls of Clyde* (1878) and *Marion Chicott* (1882).

Falls of Clyde

The *Falls of Clyde* had a distinguished career and is still with us. Launched in December 1878 by Russell and Co., Port Glasgow, she was the pioneer ship of the Glasgow 'Falls Line' (Wright and Breakenridge) and the first of six well-known iron four-masted full riggers, all of them named after Scottish waterfalls. Of 1,809gt and 1,748nt on dimensions 266.1 x 40.0 x 23.5 feet, she was initially engaged in the Calcutta jute trade – 'a noted heeler', according to Basil Lubbock, and

The *Falls of Clyde* leaving Honolulu. Neither the *Clyde* nor the *Marion Chilcott* normally used tugs, coming up to their wharf and leaving under sail. The white boiler chimney, visible near the foot of the jigger mast, was modestly sized and looked like a steamer's funnel, so that it was often asked if the vessel was an auxiliary. *[San Francisco Maritime National Historical Park H7.1,759n]*

'making no fuss at fifteen knots' according to one of her masters, Captain C. Anderson.

After 20 years under the British flag she passed into the hands of Arthur M. Brown of Honolulu, who in turn sold her to Captain Matson and associates for $25,000 on 19th December 1898. She arrived in Hawaii in January 1899, the first deepwater ship to fly the flag of the Hawaiian republic, and then in 1900 came under US registry (San Francisco) when the islands were admitted as a territory of the United States. Matson spent another $15,000 rigging her down to a four-masted barque, adding a deckhouse and charthouse, and improving her accommodation for passengers, and for nine years she carried general cargo (dry goods, livestock, automobiles, sugar-mill machinery, locomotives and railway equipment) from San Francisco to Hawaii, returning with bagged sugar.

In December 1906, as part of the Matson Navigation Company's programme of change from sail to steam, the *Falls of Clyde, Marion Chilcott, Monterey* (ex-*Cypromene*), *Santiago* and *Roderick Dhu* were sold to the Associated Oil Company of San Francisco for conversion to bulk tankers. The *Monterey, Santiago* and *Roderick Dhu* in fact simply became tank schooner barges, although the *Monterey* was refitted as a five-masted barquentine for the lumber trade in 1919, being eventually broken up at Los Angeles in 1934. The *Falls of Clyde* and *Marion Chilcott,* however, were given a new lease of life. The *Clyde* was fitted with ten tanks

The restored *Falls of Clyde* at her present berth in Honolulu. Yards and other equipment were supplied by the Lithgow shipyard, Glasgow. The new figurehead of English elm was carved in 1974 by Jack Whitehead of the British firm of Whitehead and Gaches. *[Bishop Museum]*

with a capacity of 19,160 barrels and additionally loaded 1,200 steel drums of gasoline, of 100 gallons capacity, in the 'tween decks. An oil-fired Scotch boiler in the 'tween decks supplied steam to two double-acting cargo pumps, the windlass, two winches and a generator. She carried oil to Honolulu from Santa Barbara, Gaviota and Monterey – passages which generally took two weeks and which opened up a new era in petroleum supply to the islands – returning in ballast, until 1916 when the run changed: thenceforth she traded from San Francisco with fuel oil and gasoline, returning from Honolulu with molasses.

Captain Fred K. Klebingat, who was mate of the *Clyde* in 1916-18, remembered her affectionately: ' ... *she was a handy ship in a pleasant trade, good food and good pay, considering the times ...She was never stinted for gear; coils of rope and reels of wire were there, to be used when needed...The Associated Oil Co., and especially its general manager Mr. Walter E. Buck, took great pride in the upkeep of their fleet, and especially of the* Falls of Clyde *... the mate and one watch could walk circles around her, at no time did we ever call all hands. While in the Hawaii trade she carried master, two mates, pumpman, carpenter, cook, cabin-boy and ten A.B.s. In the Atlantic she carried sixteen men before the mast. She handled like a boat, the mate and his five men on watch would have no trouble going about, but of course they had to step lively. Only beating in close quarters we would have steam up and haul the yards around with steam, and if it was night we used the electric deck-*

lights to make work easy. When I was in her the best day's run was 327 miles ...11 days from Honolulu to San Francisco ... Her best sailing point was with the wind on her beam. She travelled 12 knots very easily, and I have seen her logging 14 knots and over many a time. In the two years I was in the vessel I never saw a ship which could keep up with her' (*The Annual Dog Watch,* 1957, No.14, 58-65).

Both the *Falls of Clyde* and the *Marion Chilcott* made voyages to Europe to meet fuel shortages in the immediate post-First World War years. These were to be their swan songs. In 1920 the *Clyde* was chartered by G.W. McNear of San Francisco to take diesel oil to Denmark. Leaving the Golden Gate on 31st January she arrived at Kolding on 5th June, meeting her running mate the *Chilcott* just north of the Equator in the Atlantic, en route from San Francisco to Amsterdam, also with diesel. The *Clyde* left Kolding on 18th June 1920 on her last passage under sail: 68 days to Galveston and thence to Beaumont, and home to California via Mexico, Brazil and Argentina.

In the course of these last wanderings – in January 1921 – the *Falls of Clyde* had been acquired by the General Petroleum Corporation of California. Rigged down to a three-masted schooner barge at San Pedro, she was sent as a floating oil depot to Ketchikan, Alaska, where she remained for the next 36 years. In 1958, when there was no further use for her, it was planned to sink her as part of a breakwater at Vancouver, but a saviour intervened in the form of William Mitchell junior, who had her towed to Seattle and tried to raise interest and funds for her preservation as a floating museum. There then followed four years of endeavour by Karl Kortum, Director of the San Francisco Maritime Museum, and Captain Fred K. Klebingat. No interest was shown by Seattle, San Francisco, Los Angeles, Long Beach or San Diego, and Mitchell's bank foreclosed on him, but fortunately the old ship remained strong in the affections of the people of Hawaii. Kortum and Klebingat found champions in Honolulu historian John Wright, columnist Bob Krauss of the *Honolulu Advertiser*, and local radio stations. Public donations, including school children's collections, and donations from the Matson Navigation Company, raised $18.950 for the vessel's purchase. The *Falls of Clyde* was surveyed at Todd No.2 Dry Dock in Seattle, followed by a 20-day tow to Honolulu by the U.S. Navy tug *Moctobi*, arriving on 18th November 1963. There she has been restored by the Bernice P. Bishop Museum and the State of Hawaii. One hundred and twenty-eight years after her launch her 11/16-inch wrought iron plates have preserved for us the only restored four-masted full-rigged ship and the only surviving sailing tanker.

Marion Chilcott

The iron full rigger *Marion Chilcott* began life as the *Kilbrannan*, launched by Russell and Co. in November 1882 for Kerr, Newton and Co. of Glasgow. She measured 1,737gt and 1,510nt on dimensions 256.4 x 38.2 x 22.8 feet. On 9th February 1896 she stranded at Point Wilson, near Port Townsend, Washington State, while entering Puget Sound. Five tugs failed to pull her off and she remained aground for 11 months, her fate in doubt. Finally, a channel was dredged around her and in December 1896 she was refloated and taken into Esquimalt, where she was abandoned to the underwriters. At Quartermaster Harbour dry dock on Puget Sound 44 new plates and five new frames were installed and her keel rebuilt, and she emerged as the *Marion Chilcott*, owned by Captain Richard Chilcott, a Port Blakeley shipping agent, with a view to putting her in the lumber trade to Australia.

On 10th November 1897 she was purchased by Captain Matson and associates and, employing the same tactic as with the *Falls of Clyde*, placed temporarily under the Hawaiian flag in order to obtain United States registry upon the islands' annexation. It was while in Matson ownership that the *Chilcott* – always a smart sailer – made the record passage of 34 days from Newcastle, New South Wales to Honolulu. Sold to the National Oil and Transportation Company on 20th June 1905, by 1907 (like the *Clyde*) she was in the hands of the Associated Oil Company and was converted into a tanker with a capacity of 16,814 barrels.

Like the *Falls of Clyde*, the *Chilcott* ended her sailing-tanker career in North Atlantic waters, and with her running mate was sold – or chartered – to G.W. McNear in 1920 for trade between Gulf of Mexico ports and Europe. In 1920 she went from San Francisco to Amsterdam in 141 days and thence to Beaumont, Texas in 54 days; and the following year arrived in the Mersey from Port Arthur, Texas, again returning from Garston in 54 days. No further cargoes forthcoming, she was laid up in 1922 and in 1926 towed to Port of Spain, Trinidad, to be cut down to a molasses barge for United British Refineries Ltd. She was broken up at Port of Spain around 1954, after spending her final years as a government oil barge.

Brilliant

The sister ships *Brilliant* and *Daylight* were among the eight big sailing vessels launched 1901-3 for the Anglo-American Oil Company's case-oil trade. They were the largest sailing ships under the British flag (apart from, briefly, the five-masted barque *Neath* ex-*R.C. Rickmers* during the First World War) and the biggest four-masted barques ever built. Each costing some £54,000, they were heavily built and rigged. Water ballast tanks held 2,000 tons (case oil was sometimes a one-way trade) and the tank bulkheads greatly strengthened the hulls. Their lower yards measured 100 feet, and their royal yards 52 feet, between the plugs, and their spike bowsprits 61

The *Marion Chilcott* arrives in the Mersey in 1921, carrying her last cargo as a sailing tanker. Her oil-fired boiler and white chimney can be seen on top of the forward deckhouse. One of her cargo pumps was driven by a petrol motor, the other was steam driven. *[H.N. Cooper/J. & M. Clarkson collection]*

The *Brilliant* in the Indian Ocean, north of Durban, on passage New York-Calcutta. *[NPA/J. & M. Clarkson collection]*

feet. Their cro'jacks alone comprised 3,800 square feet of canvas. Unusually for vessels of this date and class, their topgallant masts and royal yards were of Oregon pine.

The *Brilliant* was launched in May 1901 by Russell and Co. (yard no. 475). She measured 3,765gt and 3,609nt on dimensions 352.5 x 49.1 x 28.2 feet; official number 112846 and signal letters SHJV. Able to carry 148,000 cases – the equivalent of three quarters of a million US gallons – the *Brilliant* had a crew of 46 (master, three mates, bosun, sailmaker, carpenter, donkeyman, two cooks, two stewards, six apprentices and 28 seamen) compared with the *Thomas W. Lawson*'s 16-18. With her sister she carried kerosene to the Far East; homeward cargoes when available included jute from Calcutta, tea from Hong Kong, coal from Australia and manganese ore from Vizagapatam. In 1910 the *Brilliant* and *Daylight* were converted to bulk carriers at New York. In an operation which took only six weeks, extra web frames were fitted in the 'tween decks and stiffeners on the bulkheads, and cargo pumps were fitted capable of handling 100 tons per hour.

With the break-up of the Standard Oil Company in 1911 the *Brilliant* was transferred to the Tank Storage & Carriage Company of Hong Kong, and then in July 1914 was bought by Ferdinand Laeisz of Hamburg, acting for the Deutsche-Amerikanische Petroleum Gesellschaft. Laeisz had already acquired two other components of the 1901-3 Anglo-American cohort: the four-masted barque *Arrow*, renamed *Parma* in 1911, and the full rigger *Radiant*, renamed *Perim* in 1912. Given the name *Perkeo* as she lay at New York, the ex-*Brilliant* had only the briefest career in the Flying-P Line. Under the command of Captain Hinrich Nissen, one-time master of the *Preussen* and *Potosi*, the *Perkeo* left New York for Hamburg on her delivery passage but on 6th August 1914, unaware that war had broken out, was apprehended in the Straits of Dover by the British destroyer *Zulu*. While Captain Nissen headed for five years' internment in the Isle of Man, the *Perkeo* was sold in 1915 to Alf Monsen of Tönsberg for £12,200 and renamed *Bell*. She made only one voyage under Norway's

much-abused neutral flag. Sailing from London back to New York, she then took case oil to Japan. Crossing over to Portland, Oregon, in the fast time of 24 days, she loaded wheat for the UK for orders. She was torpedoed on 30 March 1916, 70 miles south west of the Scillies, 120 days out, by U 44 (Kapitänleutnant Wagenführ). The crew were saved and brought into Liverpool.

Daylight

Following her sister from Russell's yard in January 1902 (Yard No.490, Official No.114812) the *Daylight* had a much longer career. Her dimensions differed only slightly from those of the *Brilliant* – 3,756gt and 3,599nt on measurements of 351.5 x 49.1 x 28.2 feet – but she proved to be the biggest carrier in the Anglo-American case-oil fleet: Lubbock records her loading 152,000 cases at New York in May 1907. In 1906, while still in the case-oil trade, the *Daylight* caught fire at Yokkaichi, Japan, and had to be scuttled, but was quickly raised and refitted at a local yard.

Some of these big carriers could make fast passages when they had enough wind, although naturally they could not ghost in light airs. Thus, the *Daylight* made a very smart passage in 1907 from New York to Cape Otway in 77 days, plus two days more to Williamstown; and in 1912, now a tanker, went from Hong Kong to the Delaware Capes in 87 days. On the other hand, in 1903 she took 185 days from New York to Yokohama. Trading in the Pacific, such vessels were often slowed by accumulations of sea growth: when the *Daylight* arrived at Philadelphia in 1908 after a passage of 145 days from Vizagapatam, 40 tons of barnacles were scraped off her bottom.

Captain W.E. Chapman, who served in the *Daylight* in 1903 as an AB at $18.00 per month, described her as very handy to work and a good-living ship:

' She was very heavily rigged, but being equipped with plenty of capstans and other appliances and having plenty of manpower, she was very handy to work ... in this ship, which carried a qualified donkeyman, a supply of fresh water was

made available every six weeks, so that the crew were able to indulge in the luxury of a wash every day and to wash their clothes when necessary ... The food in the Daylight *was much more varied and plentiful than Board of Trade regulations stipulated, and it was well prepared and served by the four Chinese cooks and stewards whom she carried. The forecastles for port and starboard watches were roomy and well-appointed'* (Sea Breezes, New Series, 1951:**12**;8-9).

After conversion to a tanker in 1910 and undergoing the different nominal ownerships and registrations consequent upon the break-up of Standard Oil under anti-trust legislation in 1911 (Standard Oil Company of New York/Socony 1911; Tank Storage & Carriage Co. Ltd., London, 1912; Standard Transportation Co., Hong Kong, 1914 or 1917) the *Daylight* continued to earn good dividends for 11 more years, especially during the First World War. Under Hong Kong registry she kept out of harm's way in the kerosene trade between San Francisco and the Far East. She made her last voyage as a four-masted barque in 1920-21, leaving San Francisco in October 1920 with 150,235 cases of oil for Manila and arriving back at the Golden Gate in June 1921, 71 days from Manila with 1,428 tons of copra.

With the post-war shipping slump already being felt, Standard Transportation lost no time in selling the *Daylight* to the Charles Nelson Co. of San Francisco in the summer of 1921 for the paltry sum of $22,500. Nelson's intention was to use her in the lumber trade but her deep tanks made long timber difficult to stow and she lay idle in Oakland Creek until May 1924, when she was sold to James Griffiths and Sons, ship and tug owners and brokers of Long Beach, California, and Seattle. Griffiths and Sons purchased large sailing vessels cheaply in the 1920s – including well-known ships such as the British-built *Melanope, British Merchant, Riversdale, Lord Templetown* and *Baroda*, as well as a number of US craft –

converting them to barges to carry coal, copper and concentrates between Puget Sound, northern British Columbia and Alaska, and gypsum rock from San Marcos Island, in the Gulf of California, to their works at Long Beach. The *Daylight* was stripped to her lower masts and employed in both trades until the great depression hit: from 1934 to 1941 she was laid up at Wilmslow, Washington.

War with its demand for tonnage again changed the *Daylight's* fortunes. In 1942-3 Griffiths sold her to Canadian interests, the Anglo-Canadian Shipping Company of Vancouver. She was fitted with two six-cylinder 400hp diesel engines (reputedly 20 years old) by the Skandia Oil Engine Co. of Oakland, California – devices which gave nothing but trouble during the remaining ten years of her life – and a squat funnel aft. The twin screws were supplemented by a peculiar 'barquentine' rig in which the fore mast carried a fore course, lower topsail and raffee upper topsail, while the original main, mizzen and jigger lower masts were given pole topmasts, these carrying large staysails or leg-of-mutton sails. The midships deckhouse was extended to the bulwarks and surmounted by a bridge.

In this unorthodox guise the *Daylight* left Vancouver on 25th March 1943 and Port Alberni, British Columbia, on 11th April, called at Los Angeles on 6th June, and arrived at Cape Town via Cape Horn in the creditable time of 86 days. She carried an equally unorthodox cargo of bombs, ammunition, small arms, newsprint, cement and timber, which she delivered – with delays for repairs – at Cape Town, Durban, Dar-es-Salaam and Mombasa. On 19th December 1943 she left Durban for Rio de Janeiro and on arrival on 15th January 1944, passed into the ownership of Murray, Simonsen and Co. of that port, who renamed her *Tangara* under the Brazilian flag.

Her last voyage was a chapter of accidents. In 1945 she turned up with some 2,000 tons of oil at Alexandria, Egypt,

The *Daylight* in the Delaware River, 6th November1912. *{John Dubas/Author's collection}*

where engine repairs kept her for two years. In January 1948 she left Split, Yugoslavia, with 5,000 tons of cement for Rio de Janeiro, only to limp into Naples after seven days with further engine trouble. Thence she took 21 days to Gibraltar, for stores and bunkers, and finally arrived in Rio after another 44 days, on 6th April 1948. On 20th May 1948 she left Rio in tow for Porto Alegre, her engines disabled, and thereafter seems to have spent most of her time laid up as an economic liability. She was broken up in 1953-4.

Postscript

This review has confined itself to European and American vessels, but there are other instances of the carriage of oil in bulk by sailing craft: by Chinese junks; on the Irrawaddy to Rangoon; and especially on the Black Sea, the Caspian and the Volga. In the 1870s the Swedish Nobel brothers introduced double-containment tank sailers there and by 1885 half the Caspian oil-carrying capacity consisted of converted schooners; these numbered around 212 by 1900.

No mention has been made of 'The Horse and Cart of the Atlantic' – the steam tanker *Iroquois* and its six-masted schooner-rigged towing barge *Navahoe*, an extraordinary partnership which lasted for 23 years, from 1908 to 1930. This unique arrangement is described in I. Taphouse, *Spirit of the Iroquois* (Pentland, 1995). Too late for inclusion in Part 1 of this study, there came to our notice the iron brigantine *Novelty*, built at Boston in 1869 to carry molasses in bulk from the West Indies (*Log Chips*, October 1953:3,No.7;76).

By the time steam tankers began to appear in the 1880s and 1890s, sailing tankers had been trading for a quarter of a century and the powered vessels benefited from their experience in the safe transport of petroleum by sea – transverse and longitudinal bulkheads, expansion tanks, pressure systems to control expansion. At first it was thought prudent to keep oil cargoes away from coal-fired boilers, and in any event the shipping of cheap bulk cargoes by steamer was uneconomic prior to the introduction of the triple expansion engine. The first ocean-going tank steamer – the 2,748gt *Vaderland*, launched by Palmers of Newcastle on 21st August 1872 for the Red Star Line of Antwerp to carry passengers as well as oil on a regular New York-Antwerp service – ran into trouble almost immediately because the US authorities would not allow passengers to be carried in such conditions, while the Antwerp officials would not permit storage tanks to be constructed in the port. Excluding the Nobel brothers' *Zoroaster* of 1878, the prototype of the modern powered tanker is generally reckoned to be the 2,307gt *Glückauf*, built by Armstrong Whitworth of Newcastle for the Deutsche-Amerikanische Petroleum Gesellschaft (Wilhelm Anton Riedemann, the same enterprising ship owner who converted the composite full rigger *Andromeda* in 1885) and she was not launched until 1886. It was the increasing size of steam-powered tankers which put paid to the sailing tanker. By the early twentieth century 8,000dwt steamers were the norm, rising to 12,000dwt by the First World War – sizes with which sailing vessels could not compete in handling ability.

Besides their reputation for handling badly and safety fears, sailing tankers were unpopular with crews because of their quick turn-round in port. In the *Quévilly*'s first year of service, even though they were paid more than the normal wages in French sailing ships, some 100 crew members passed through the vessel, giving an average service of only four months. Captain Jonathan W. Dunham, master of Standard Oil's case-oil carrier *Astral*, remarked in a letter of November 1908: '… the Company thinks of having a fleet of tank sailing ships. In this case they would never be in port … over one or two days at a time … they would never get captains or officers to stay over one voyage, this would mean being at sea all the time' (W.H. Bunting, *Sea Struck*, Tilbury House, Gardiner, Maine, 2004, 309).

Nevertheless, sailing tankers endured up to the 1920s. It was ironic that the lives of some of the last big deepwater sailing vessels were prolonged by transporting the fuel which was hastening their demise.

SOURCES AND ACKNOWLEDGEMENTS

We thank all who gave permission for their photographs to be used, and for help in finding photographs we are particularly grateful to Tony Smith, Jim McFaul and David Whiteside of the World Ship Photo Library; to Ian Farquhar, F.W. Hawks, Peter Newall, Ivor Rooke, William Schell, George Scott; and to David Hodge and Bob Todd of the National Maritime Museum, and other museums and institutions listed.

Research sources have included the *Registers* of William Schell and Tony Starke, *Lloyd's Register*, *Lloyd's Confidential Index*, *Lloyd's War Losses*, *Mercantile Navy Lists*, *Marine News* and *Shipbuilding and Shipping Record*. Use of the facilities of the World Ship Society's Central Record, the Guildhall Library, the Public Record Office and Lloyd's Register of Shipping are gratefully acknowledged, and Dr Malcolm Cooper is thanked for checking Second World War losses. Particular thanks also to Heather Fenton

for editorial and indexing work, and to Marion Clarkson for accountancy services.

Fleet in Focus: Palm Line
The history of the company and its predecessors has been covered in 'Palm Line: the Coming of Age' by Roger Kohn (Palm Line Limited, London, 1970) and 'Palm Line' by Laurence Dunn and Paul Heaton (P.M. Heaton, Abergavenny, 1994). Much of the material in this chapter is based on accounts in the technical press, especially 'Shipping and Shipbuilding Record' and 'The Motorship'.

J. Wharton (Shipping) Ltd.
This history was commenced a number of years ago during which time many people and organisations have been consulted and the author extends his grateful thanks to the following, with apologies for anyone who has helped and has been omitted.
The Registrars at Goole, Hull, London,

Lerwick, Newcastle-upon-Tyne, Southampton, Dundee, Cardiff, Gibraltar, Dublin, Limassol, St.Vincent, Piraeus and the Registrar General.
Lloyd's Register, Germanischer Lloyd, Hellenic Register, Bureau Veritas, Nederlandse Scheepvaart Inspectie.
The National Archives, Guildhall Library, County Record Office, Beverley, City of Wakefield Archives, Scunthorpe Public Library.
World Ship Society, Great Central Railway Society, Keel and Lighter Owners Mutual Insurance and Protecting Society, British Waterways.
M. Banavage, J. Burtt, M. Cassar, C. Conway, A. Cowne, Dr.J. Fairbank, J. Goodchild, F. Harlington, H. Higgs, D. Hocquard, B. Jones, C. Knowles, N. Koutouvalis, B. Kruidhof, B. Longbone, E. Paget-Tomlinson, M. Schuster, S. Smith, L. Spurling, D. Tyneman, S. Wharton, G. Winter.

RECORD REVIEWS

REUBEN CHAPPELL: PIERHEAD PAINTER by Robert Jones
160 page hardback published by First Light at £29.99.
Reuben Chappell was certainly the most prolific, and probably the most technically proficient, of the British pierhead painters, that band of artists who produced fast, technically accurate and affordable portraits of ships for sale to members of their crews. Based at Goole and later Par, Chappell painted mainly sailing and steam coasters, often providing the only known image of many craft which did not survive long enough to be photographed. This is the first major book on Chappell, and few publications have been so eagerly awaited by this reviewer. And few have disappointed him so thoroughly.

The first thing one would ask from a celebration of a painter's work is good colour reproduction. Yet a significant proportion of the images in this book are washed out and pale. The original watercolours might have faded but, given Chappell's incredible output, enough have survived in good condition which could have been chosen instead. The problem is more likely defective scanning, reproduction, or manipulation - a failing the Italian printers should never have been allowed to get away with by the publisher. This is just not good enough for a £30 book.

Neither is there an excuse for the errors in the text. For his information, the author has relied on previously published work, quite probably on some written by this reviewer. No problem with that, but the author has not even been able to copy accurately, and names of builders and owners are garbled, managers confused with owners, facts are distorted, and some of it is just made up. For instance, in half a lifetime of researching steam coasters this reviewer has never heard of a 'transitional' period of design, apparently when they carried sails. In fact, they did this from the genesis of steam bulk carriers in the 1850s until the First World War – hardly a 'transitional' period. Typographical, spelling and punctuation errors and inconsistencies abound. Even the subject's name is spelt wrongly in places.

The author is himself an artist, and although he provides some interesting images from Chappell's notebooks, nowhere do we get an insight into just how Chappell achieved an output on an industrial scale, estimated at an incredible 12,000 paintings. In his busiest years he was producing these small masterpieces at a rate of ten every week, and that was without working on Sundays. A list of known surviving examples of Chappell's work might have deflected some of this reviewer's ire, but this does not appear.

Is there anything good about the book? The biography of Chappell is useful, although it could have done without some of the padding. When the printers bothered to get them right, i.e. in about half the examples, the reproductions of Chappell's paintings are good to have. The accompanying photographs are usually well chosen and mostly well reproduced, although captioning could be better and permission for reproduction has not always been sought.

Sadly, given the limited market for maritime books, and the cost of colour images, it is unlikely that anyone else will publish on Reuben Chappell. A pity, as this important artist and the ships he recorded so accurately deserve better than this flawed, amateurish effort.
Roy Fenton

MERSEY DOCKS FLEET LIST compiled by Gordon F. Wright
58-page softback published by Countyvise Limited for the Liverpool Nautical Research Society at £7.50
Dredgers and other harbour craft are important, but hardly sexy craft, and very little has ever been published, especially on the careers of such craft. The authorities responsible for the Mersey had a large, varied and fascinating fleet, and the Liverpool Nautical Research Society (LNRS) is to be congratulated on recording it in this book.

There is a rather brief overview of the history of the Mersey authorities and their dredging activities, followed by a fleet list of all the vessels they have owned, well over 300. The data recorded are names, official numbers, dates, builders, engines and dimensions. The column for the vessels' history lists the type, then gives dates acquired and sold, usually with details of owners before and after it worked on the Mersey. The histories have evidently been researched from the Liverpool registration documents held in the Merseyside Maritime Museum. This is admirable, but the histories of a number of craft are taken little further than the closure of their Liverpool registry. In most such cases it would not have required a great deal of further work to have completed the craft's history: after all, it is by a *research* society.

The scans of photographs are reasonably well reproduced, which is all that can be expected in a limited-run publication. But that is no reason to have allowed the bows or sterns of some vessels to have been cut off when Countyvise prepared them for publication. Printers often try to get away with this, but can usually be persuaded to do better.

This is the sort of information that needs to be published, and societies like the LNRS are well suited to doing so: they can enhance their image and encourage their members by making their research more widely available. However, the LNRS should have been more ambitious, demanding a little more from the researchers and from their printers. Nevertheless, it is an admirable effort.
Roy Fenton

SCOTT LITHGOW: DÉJÀ VU ALL OVER AGAIN! THE RISE AND FALL OF A SHIPBUILDING COMPANY by Lewis Johnman and Hugh Murphy (Research in Maritime History No. 30)
364-page softback published by the International Maritime Economic History Association, St. John's, Newfoundland at £30.00
With only a brief yard list, and few photographs, this is clearly an academic history book but, as the title signals, it is not written in an academic style. Indeed it is a book anyone with an interest in the history of British shipbuilding should read.

Scott Lithgow and its predecessors were hugely significant Clyde shipbuilders, which meant that for much of their history they were internationally important. The Lithgow family, in particular, were highly influential, being instrumental in setting up, for example, the highly controversial National Shipbuilders Security Limited which 'sterilised' many shipyards in the interwar years. Whilst Scott's yard successfully built both merchant ships and naval, and were submarine specialists, Lithgows succeeded by concentrating on standard tramp ships, generating wealth which saw the family control Fairfields at Govan and major engine builders such as David Rowan and Kincaids. But even with this experience and wealth, it all went very wrong. Merger, nationalisation and then reprivatisation saw the combined Scott-Lithgow yard involved in the most expensive disaster in British shipbuilding, the drilling rig *Ocean Alliance*, on which the loss was an almost unimaginable £211,000,000.

The book begins with a history of each of the constituent yards, Scotts of Greenock and Russell and Company and its successor Lithgows Ltd. The emphasis is more on the financial history of the concerns, their performance as shipbuilders, and relationships with customers than on the yards' outputs in terms of individual ships, but these are not neglected. The second and slightly longer part deals with what led up to the merger and its aftermath. This story, especially the aftermath, is a heady one, which the authors clearly relish telling. From it no-one emerges with much credit: politicians, the Admiralty, management, unions and consultants. The book is clearly a result of a monumental piece of research, both in the records of the builders and in government archives.

The aim of the book is to examine what went wrong with British shipbuilding by looking at one particularly important example. In this it succeeds admirably, and anyone reading it will appreciate how the British industry, which seemed unassailable as recently as 1920, could become a basket case a few decades later. It may well also alter your view of how shipbuilding histories should be written.
Roy Fenton

PUTTING THE RECORD STRAIGHT

Letters, additions, amendments and photographs relating to features in *any* issues of 'Record' are welcomed. Letters may be edited. Communications by e-mail are welcome, but senders are asked to include their postal address.

Alice in Norway

Referring to John Naylon's excellent article on sailing tankers in 'Record 34', I have some minor comments, mainly on the *Alice et Isabelle* of 1893. True, the vessel was sold in June 1910 to A/S Vallø Olieraffineri, an early oil refinery located between the town of Tønsberg and the present Esso Slagen Refinery on the Oslo Fjord. This company belonged to the Standard Oil (Esso) empire, as did its successor, Østlandske Petroleumscompagni in Oslo and the affiliated Vestlandske Petroleums Co. in Bergen (the owners of *Unionen* and later *Snespurven* (ex *Rendova*), mentioned in the same article). Incidentally, the first steam tanker to come under Norwegian register was the *Oranje Prince* of 1889, acquired by Vallø Olieraffinerie in 1907 and renamed *Helios*; only to be lost at sea in March 1908.

In March 1912, the *Alice et Isabelle* was sold to Det Danske Petroleums A/S, Copenhagen, and converted into the tank barge *Dieselea*. By 1918 she was re-rigged as barque for the same owners and given the name *Astrid*, according to the DNV register. Her renaissance as a sailing vessel was short-lived, and in January 1923 the vessel, again as a barge, was sold to the merchants Christian von Tangen A/S, Bergen. Little is known about her whereabouts; sold back to J.C. Giertsen of Copenhagen in 1925, but again to Norway in August 1926, to Norsk Tankanlaeg A/S, Oslo (the local BP affiliate) as the tank barge *Mil 15*.

Late in 1939 she was hired by the Royal Norwegian Navy as a stationary oil depot, lying at Svolvaer in the Lofoten islands. When the royal family, the cabinet and the remaining part of the armed forces had to withdraw from northern Norway on 7th June 1940 and go into exile in the UK, the *Mil 15* was left behind at Ramfjordnes. Here she was seized by the Germans and did not survive the war.
DAG BAKKA Junior, Haugeveien 31, NO-5005 Bergen, Norway dbakka@online.no

Metacentres: last words (and numbers)

I'm not sure if you want anyone adding to the mist surrounding the metacentre, but they do say the exception proves the rule.

In 1980 I had the dubious privilege of being the mate of a drill ship in the Beaufort Sea. The ship had started life as a C1-M-AV1 with the unlovely name of *Snake Hitch*. When converted to a drill ship wing tanks were added over most of the length of the hull, greatly increasing her beam. Later additional sponsons were added amidships for storing bulk supplies, and increasing the beam to 100 feet (the length being 377 feet), which had a dramatic effect on the metacentric height.

In this ship's case M was, as John Goble mentions, up near the cross-trees, or at least up in the drill tower. Conventionally, if you add weight low down, G - the centre of gravity - will be lowered and the GM increased providing an increased righting lever, GZ. However, in this oddly-shaped ship an anomolous situation arose once the draft passed 19 feet 6 inches. Adding weight in the double bottom tanks did lower G, but it lowered M at a far greater rate, resulting in a reduced GM and correspondingly smaller righting lever. For example: KM 47.95 feet; KG 31; 82 feet; fluid GM 15.37 feet. Conventional 10,000 ton cargo ships usually had a GM somewhere between 1-3 feet. Some food for Archimedean thought in the bath for aging seafarers!
Captain JOHN ANDERSON, 523 Louise Road, Ladysmith, British Columbia, V9G 1W7, Canada

Putting 34 straight

'Record' 34 arrived today and I have been having a good time looking through it.

On page 84 – I know what the post card says, but Bureau Veritas classed her and they seem to be of the opinion that she was named *Alice Isabelle*, not *Alice et Isabelle*, at least in their 1911 Register Book. She is *Alice Isabelle* for her entire life in 'Lloyd's Register'.

On page 87 – I don't think the *Sunlight* was in Sydney in that picture, it looks an awful lot like the east side of the Fort Point Channel in Boston, perhaps about 400

Hibernian Coast (1,258/ 1947), one of the ships on which George Osbon may possibly have taken passage around the United Kingdom. Completed as the *Aberdonian Coast* by Hall Russell and Co. Ltd, for Coast Lines Ltd, she was renamed *Hibernian Coast in 1948.* In September 1968 she was sold to Kuwait buyers and renamed *Port Said Coast.* Her end came in May 1974 when she was sold to Spanish breakers at Cartagena. *[J. and M. Clarkson collection]*

yards closer to the entrance than where the *Dallington* was photographed at the Domino Sugar Refinery (page 93). I would swear the roof-top water tank towards the left side of the picture reads 'Necco' - the same water tank is at the left edge of the picture of the *Dallington*. 'Necco' was the New England Confectionary Co. – best known for their rolls of pastel multi-coloured 'Necco Wafers' (a candy that as a child I viewed as something of a disappointment, but consumed anyway). The 'oil' storage tank is in all probability holding molasses. For the record that photo of the *Dallington* was taken by the late Richard Hildebrand on 8th April 1913.

Page 127. *Firdausa* – the suggestion that she was broken up at Gadani Beach is anachronistic as the earliest possible reference to beach breaking outside Karachi that I have seen is in 1969. The entry in the 'Lloyd's Wreck Book' said she was sold to Carstairs and Cumming Ltd., who began work at Karachi in April 1963. The first record of an instance of beach breaking in Pakistan would seem to be the scrapping of the Lebanese *Evangelos* (3,911/1918): 'Marine News' reported her sale to Sind Steel Corporation and said she had been beached about 20 miles west of Karachi prior to 23.10.69 for scrapping. Even then that would appear to be Somiani Beach, where the *Chittagong City* was scrapped in 1971. I don't believe Gadani came into use until Pakistani buyers began large scale importation of ships for scrap about 1974.

Having said this I have looked at the article a bit more and find widespread references to Gadani Beach - for the record here is what I have for the ships in question.
Firoza: broken up at Karachi by Dodhy and Co., work began about 11.10.1960.
Kaderbaksh: broken up at Karachi by Carstairs and Cumming Ltd., December 1961.
Mustali: broken up at Karachi by Sind Steel Corporation, September 1960.
Fakirjee Cowasjee: broken up at Karachi by Hardware Manufacturing Co.; reported sold June 1967, work began in December 1967.
Ocean Endeavour: broken up at Karachi by Mohammedi Rolling Mills, work began in February 1967.

Chittagong City: sold to Bakshi and Co., Karachi; work began 15.4.1971 at Somiani Beach, 23 miles from Karachi.
Feronia: broken up at Karachi by Hardware Manufacturing and Shipbreakers Ltd.; work began 12.9.70.
BILL SCHELL, 334 So. Franklin Street Holbrook MA, USA

Kerry clarification

From various views of ships in the Mersey I am satisfied that the *Kerry* is seen on that river ('Record' 33, page 29). She was trading there from Dublin, principally with cattle and returning with general cargo. Neither one of her deck officers at the time nor anyone else recalls her making the 600 nautical mile trip to London. Being a steamer and not fitted with radar she would hardly be suitable or economical given also that Coast Lines then had an extensive fleet of motor ships including those maintaining the Liverpool to London route which also took in Dublin (the old British and Irish service).

Everards' tankers were not unknown on the Mersey but another pointer is that she is flying her pilot exemption flag, her officers being required to have their Dublin and Liverpool pilotage certificates.

While George Osbon seems to have principally taken ships on the Thames, I have seen views taken elsewhere. These lead me to suggest that, just maybe, he took a passenger berth on the *Hibernian Coast* or *Caledonian Coast* as the photos in my collection show, for example, the *Theano* of the Holland-Ireland Line crossing Dublin Bay and the Lubeck steamer *Fona* alongside at North Wall, Dublin. Based on the trading patterns of the ships of which I have photos I would suggest that, armed with a camera, he made a trip from London in the late 1950s. This would explain the locations of some of these photos.
TERRY Ó CONALLÁIN, 3 The Park, Skerries Road, Skerries, County Dublin, Ireland.

Bristol City corrections

Small point for the record. The *Montreal City* was in convoy ON.152 not ONS.152 and indeed a straggler. The

ONS series did not start until March 1943. Prior to this ON convoys were of two types, fast and slow. It was common practice to call the slow ON convoys ON(S) but as far as the Admiralty were concerned they were ON convoys, and can be shown this is so by reading archive material. Axis Submarine Successes has loads of entries for ONS convoys but prior to 1943 these are all incorrect.

The *Montreal City* was sunk in a surface attack by *U 591* which first fired a three-torpedo spread which missed. A single shot later struck the ship aft, followed by a final hit amidships. The boat went to the lifeboats to identify the ship they had attacked; there were three boat loads of survivors, but none survived. According to the war diary of *U 591* the sea where she sank was littered with empty oil barrels.
DAVID SIBLEY, Moorcroft, Castle Lane, East Ayton, Scarborough, YO13 9EN

As usual the standards of 'Record' 32 and 33 are second to none and I am particularly impressed by the superb quality of the colour sections. I was very interested in the Bristol City Line history as I remember so well their ships from the late-1950s until they ceased. For the record though, just a few small mistakes I noticed in the fleet history section: both *Montreal City* and *Halifax City* are reported as laid up in 1972 at Swansea, but actually it was No. 2 Dock, Barry; they were also both handed over at Barry to their new Thai owner. *Halifax City* had been renamed *Thonburi* in December 1972, not *Thornbury* in 1973. Thai livery, sporting a black hull with red boot topping; close by the *Ratchaburi* also had been similarly repainted.
NIGEL JONES, 12 Powys Drive, Dinas Powys, CF64 4LN

Springfjord's sister
The story of *Springfjord* ('The donkeyman's tale, 'Record' 32) was of particular interest to me, being a citizen of Trondheim and still remembering the launch of this vessel on 11th November 1939. In fact, Springwell Shipping Co. Ltd. ordered two identical vessels from Trondhjems Mekaniska Verksted, yard numbers 208 and 209. The name of the second one would have been *Springsound*, but this vessel was – like the first – transferred to DDG Hansa and given the name *Nierstein* when launched on 17th September 1940. The German owners did not fulfil their obligations on either of the two ships, and *Nierstein* was sold in unfinished condition to local Trondheim owners Det Nordenfjeldske Dampskibsselskab. On 24th February 1943 she was towed to Fredrikstad Mekaniske Verksted to be completed. On its first voyage on 25th July 1943 the vessel

was bombed and sunk alongside the quay at Hamburg. In November 1943 it was raised and towed back to Fredrikstad to be repaired, not being completed until February 1947 and delivered to Det Nordenfjeldske Dampskibsselskab and named *Svein Jarl* according to the usual nomenclature of the company. It had, however, a short life as it struck a mine on 16th January 1948 near Patras whilst on a voyage from Calamata to Patras with general cargo. Nine of her crew lost their lives.
TORE NILSEN, Sandbakkveien 67, N-7072 Heimdal, Norway

Regent at Foyers
In 'Record' 34 is a very nice photo of the schooner *Regent* at Foyers Jetty, Loch Ness. She was built at Montrose by Birnie in 1862, 101 gross and 80 net, ultimately registered at Inverness on 12th April 1880. On 7th September 1905 she sprang a leak and whilst on a voyage from Teignmouth to Liverpool with china clay, was towed in and condemned. In 1904 she had been re-rigged as a ketch and her last owner was Captain William Pascoe of Newquay. I just love the tracklaying in the foreground of the photo. I don't think it would pass muster with today's health and safety inspectors!
MARTIN BENN, 2 Lonsdale Mews, Croston Road, Lostock Hall, Preston PR5 5NH
According to the 'Mercantile Navy List', Regent was sold by Donald Macgregor of Inverness to Kircudbright owners in 1896, so the photograph was probably taken before that date. She was sold to Pascoe in 1902. Ed.

Active rudder aids *Rover*
The story on *Elizabeth Bowater* showing the Pleuger Aktiv rudder on page 97 of 'Record' 34 brought back memories of an older Bowater ship, the steamer *Liverpool Rover*, which was built in 1929 as *Markland* for the Markland Shipping Company of Liverpool, Nova Scotia. When I was seaman aboard her in 1956 she also had a Pleuger Aktiv rudder. I was told it had been installed to aid the steering of the twin-screw ship when passing through a narrow bridge on the Bras d'or Lakes in Cape Breton, Nova Scotia. Bowater may have gotten the idea from the older ship.
HUBERT HALL, Yarmouth, Nova Scotia B5A 4B4

Spidola
Mr Alan Pritchard of Holyhead has kindly sent to us a distant view of the **Spidola** ('Records' 31 and 32) taken at Holyhead after her grounding in 1948. The coaster alongside is no doubt off-loading some or all of her cargo. Thank you Alan.

Svein Jarl on trials near Trondheim.

FROM THE BOSUN'S LOCKER
John Clarkson

When you go out looking for interesting photographs you never know what you will come across and a recent visit to a card fair in Chester unearthed two out-of-the-usual items, one a photo the other a ticket.

The photo (right) is of officers posing on board the *Trecarrell* which must be the ship completed in 1907 and lost in 1916. Although she did not feature in 'Hain in a Hundred' in 'Record' 35 I felt this may be of interest to some readers as it shows how the officers of a tramp steamer dressed at that time. No doubt this is an 'off duty' picture and day-to-day working clothes would be much plainer and more serviceable. A note on the back tells us that from left to right are the Captain, Second Mate, Chief Mate, Third Engineer and 'myself' with the Chief Engineer sitting down. What rank 'myself' held we do not know as the lower parts of his sleeves are hidden. Quite possibly he was the Second Engineer.

The ticket is much older, dating back to 1823. I hope this will reproduce well enough for the small print to be read, but basically it is an invitation for friends of Mr Jeffery Dennis, who wishes to improve conditions in the merchant service, to dine with him at the Albion Tavern in Aldersgate Street. As the tickets were all of twelve shillings each, this would seem to be a money-raising venture. A great deal of work has gone into preparing the tickets as they have been individually numbered, the flag coloured in, and the wax seal applied bearing what looks like Mr. Dennis's initials. Whether or not there is any significance in the colours of the flag we do not know but from top to bottom they are navy blue, green, light green or grey and brown with the jack in red.

It is possible one of our readers may know more about Mr Dennis and whether or not he was able to contribute to improving conditions in the merchant service of the time.

Huntingdon's mainmast.
John B. Hill has a query about Federal Lines *Huntingdon* of 1946. Photographs of this ship are in the World Ship Society's 'Crossed Flags' and in their book on P. & O., also in 'New Zealand and Federal Lines' published by Ships in Focus. Only in the last named book is the ship shown without her mainmast. John asks when and why was the mainmast removed? Other ships in the class do not appear to have been altered.
Looking through our own dated negatives of Huntingdon *the last one with her mainmast still standing was taken in June 1965. The next one of her, taken in September 1966 shows her without a mainmast. We now know roughly when but the question of why remains. JC.*

Photographs in 'Record' 34
The first picture for identification in 'Record' 34 was easily identified - the old bosun has to make it easy sometimes - but it was the replies about the clipper-bowed ship (2/34) which surprised the old lad. We thought being a fairly small ship there would be no feedback. Little was expected regarding the freighter (3/34) with black hull and yellow funnel - too many of them about in their time - but there was just a chance someone had seen the same picture but with details of her name. To me the surprise was the coaster, being comparatively modern I felt sure we would have some answers.

1/34. This was readily identified by Craig Carter, A.D. Frost, John B. Hill, Geoff Holmes, Tony Smythe and Peter

THE FRIENDS OF Mr. JEFFERY DENNIS,
DESIROUS OF ESTABLISHING
His Systematic Plan
FOR BETTERING
THE CONDITION OF THE MERCHANT SERVICE,
WILL DINE AT
The Albion Tavern, Aldersgate Street,
On FRIDAY, JANUARY 24, 1823, *at Five o'Clock.*

TICKET, 12 SHILLINGS.

Stewards.

J. ROOME, Esq.	A. BERGH, Esq.
J. LILLEY, Esq.	THOMAS HILL, Esq.
R. WEIR, Esq. R. N.	J. M'BEAN, Esq.
CAPTAIN SCOTT.	LIEUT. GREEN, R. N.
CAPTAIN Wm. CLIFTON.	J. M. DAVISON, Esq. R.N.
JOHN DICKINSON, Esq.	T. ROOME, Esq.
JOHN BIGG, Esq.	

Wynne as showing the majority of Royal Mail's *Lochmonar* after she had been salved following grounding on the revetment at Taylor's Bank in the Crosby Channel due to a steering gear failure on 30th November 1927. She is lying in North West No.1 Branch of Canada Dock.

2/34. Identification of this clipper-bowed steamer comes from both Tony Smythe and Peter King and leaves no doubt that the vessel is the one-time *Wollowra* of the Adelaide Steamship Co. Ltd., built at Jarrow in 1891. Peter has found no fewer than five images of the ship in Australian ownership and, although there are subtle differences between each of these and 2/34, all are explainable as being due to likely modifications, especially to her boat stowage and rigging.

This ship had an interesting career, beginning life in 1891 as an Italian-registered cargo ship, operating a service between Italy and a wharf near Tower Bridge in the Thames intended to carry fruit with a subsidy from the Italian government. Sir Charles Palmer, head of the yard that built the ships, was chairman of the company, but the venture failed and its four ships were put up for sale The gold rush to Western Australia in the 1890s meant that Adelaide Steamship was desperate for new tonnage, and sent its secretary to the UK to buy what he could. So urgent was the need that *Silvio Spaventa* and her sister ship *Francesco Crispi* were bought, although they needed conversion for the passenger trade. They were renamed *Wollowra* and *Marloo*, initially operating between Sydney (where they were registered) and Fremantle. As the gold rush faded, the ships were transferred to the east coast, running between Fremantle and Cairns. *Marloo* was wrecked on this service in September 1914, and *Wollowra* sold soon afterwards.

More problematical is at what stage of her career she is depicted in 2/34. She is evidently post-conversion to a passenger ship, and has lost the yards on her foremast shown in several illustrations in Australian ownership. The star on her funnel rules out Adelaide Steamship as owners, so she must be in Hong Kong, Chinese or Spanish ownership following her sale in 1915. Tony Smythe favours Chinese ownership. Her career details are given below, courtesy of Bill Schell's register for 1891. Suggestions as to which owner put the star on her funnel are welcomed.

SILVIO SPAVENTA/WOLLOWRA/IBERIA
O.N. 104811   2,631g 1,678n 323.0 x 40.3 x 17.2 feet
T. 3-cyl. by Palmers' Shipbuilding and Iron Co. Ltd., Newcastle-upon-Tyne; 483 NHP, 12 knots.
9.1891: Completed by Palmers' Shipbuilding and Iron Co. Ltd., Newcastle-upon-Tyne (Yard No. 658) for the Italo-Britannica Royal Italian Mail Steam Navigation Co. Ltd. (E. & E. Arbib, managers), Naples as SILVIO SPAVENTA.
1893: Galbraith, Pembroke and Co. became managers.
1895: Sold to the Adelaide Steamship Co. Ltd., Adelaide, South Australia and renamed WOLLOWRA.
1915: Sold to the Wollowra Steamship Co. Ltd. (Moller and Co., managers), Hong Kong.
1917: A.R. Burkhill and Sons became managers.
1921: Sold to Chan Pan Chee, Shanghai, China.
1922: Sold to Maritima Peninsular Ltda. (Ceferino Molina, manager), Vigo, Spain and renamed IBERIA
1928: Broken up by Stavanger Skibsophugnings Co. A/S at Stavanger

3/34. Apart from suggestions that the number of side doors and ventilators indicate she is a livestock carrier, no one has even guessed at the identity of this vessel. Also could she have been loading bananas or a similar fruit cargo – often done from barges or lighters through side ports.

The Maritime Information Association
We are pleased to give a gentle plug for the Maritime Information Association, a society for everyone who deals with information about ships and other maritime matters. The MIA exists to foster a community of those using and providing such information, from researchers, historians, enthusiasts, and publishers, right through to librarians, archivists and curators. The MIA offers a forum to exchange ideas through face-to-face contacts, through its newsletter 'Maritime Informer', an annual conference, a website with an on-line forum, and with occasional visits and social events. Above all, the MIA offers a friendly way for busy people to keep in touch with each other. Further information about the MIA and a membership form will be found on www.maritime-information.net Details of membership are also available from Michael Naxton, 'Whistlers'. 6 The Mount, Caversham, Reading RG4 7RU, United Kingdom.

The MIRAMAR index: another plug
As frequent searchers for information on ships, we have been hugely impressed by the Miramar Ship Index, compiled by Rodger Haworth and sponsored by the New Zealand Ship and Marine Society, which recently went on-line on its website www.miramarshipindex.org.nz. Access is free, and the content invaluable, containing entries on 207,600 ships and 340,600 names. It provides a search facility which, on a name being entered, provides a list of candidates with details which enable a particular vessel to be identified, including date of build and tonnage. Clicking on a name brings up a Single Ship Report, which gives more detail, including builders, dimensions, changes of name and fate. Many entries are referenced to the Starke/Schell registers, in which the website's author is a partner (with Bill Schell, of Boston, U.S.A.), and which are marketed by arrangement with the World Ship Society. These registers give full ownership details.

Rodger is busy adding to his database, increasing the detail and the coverage, but our experience shows it is already very useful. For example, when searching for a dozen post-war ships in a hurry the Miramar Index gave much of the information we were looking for, and saved hours of time tracking the vessel's name changes and fates. Well done Rodger, your Herculean labours have provided an invaluable resource.

1/35: We have made a high resolution scan of the forward part of this ship and then blown them up. I would say there are six letters in the name and they may read *Capera* but I cannot trace any ship of this name. It is possible she has seven letters in her name as a mark on the bow could be damage to her paintwork or a further letter. The photo was take by W. Newark Lewis of Port Talbot .

2/35: A ship in dock which has rolled over onto her side. But what ship and where is she?

There are no clues on the back of the photograph and no names can be read on the barges or the tug in attendance.

3/35: This photo is said to be of the *Statesman* and is dated November 1915.

The only *Statesman* we can find is the Harrison Line vessel, completed in 1895 and lost in 1916 - but she had four masts and her profile was much different. Harrison's next ship of the name was completed in 1914 as the *Saint George* for Rankin, Gilmour and Co. Ltd. and renamed *Statesman* in 1918.

Has anyone any ideas?

4/35: Not a good clear picture to say the least but what is she?

Looking at the fitting near to the bow, and the overall appearance of the ship this must be a First World War photo. There are plenty of marks on the paintwork but no name, or part thereof, can be seen.